Cuba at the Crossroads

Edited by

Philip Brenner
American University

John M. Kirk
Dalhousie University

William M. LeoGrande
American University

ROWMAN & LITTLEFIELD
Lanham • Boulder • New York • London

Executive Editor: Susan McEachern
Assistant Editor: Katelyn Turner
Higher Education Channel Manager: Jonathan Raeder

Credits and acknowledgments for material borrowed from other sources, and reproduced
with permission, appear on the appropriate pages within the text.

Published by Rowman & Littlefield
An imprint of The Rowman & Littlefield Publishing Group, Inc.
4501 Forbes Boulevard, Suite 200, Lanham, Maryland 20706
https://rowman.com

6 Tinworth Street, London SE11 5AL, United Kingdom

British Library Cataloguing in Publication Information Available

Library of Congress Control Number: 2020930270

ISBN 9781538136812 (cloth : alk. paper) | ISBN 9781538136829 (pbk. : alk. paper) |
ISBN 9781538136836 (epub)

∞ ™ The paper used in this publication meets the minimum requirements of American
National Standard for Information Sciences Permanence of Paper for Printed Library
Materials, ANSI/NISO Z39.48-1992.

Contents

Preface

When Rowman & Littlefield published *A Contemporary Cuba Reader: The Revolution under Raúl Castro*, a book we edited with Marguerite Rose Jiménez in 2014, we expected President Castro's second and final term would involve knitting together the several components of a changed landscape so that he could turn over to his successor a fully revitalized Cuban Revolution. He had put in place institutional and legal reforms for governing in a way that would provide greater freedom for individuals—such as the right to travel outside Cuba and to operate small businesses—and for restructuring the economy in a way that placed the country on a path toward the goal of development with equity for all. In addition, internationally, Cuba had strong support from Russia, China, and Venezuela, despite the death of Hugo Chávez in 2013. It also was serving as the co-chair of the Economic Community of Latin America and the Caribbean (CELAC in the Spanish acronym), a recently formed and potentially influential organization whose members included every Western Hemisphere country except Canada and the United States. Improved relations with Europe and the United States appeared to be on the horizon as well.

Miguel Díaz-Canel took office as Cuba's new president in 2018. This transition seemed the appropriate moment for us to consider editing a third edition of *A Contemporary Cuba Reader* (the first edition came out in 2007). Yet Cuba was still very much in flux. Our 2014 expectations had been upended by domestic factors that had stalled the planned "updating" of Cuba's economy, by the decision to reorganize governing structures and establish new rights with a revised constitution, and by a changed international context that created several new sources of pressure on and danger for Cuba.

We have traveled to Cuba several times over the past six years, and have described and analyzed the country in articles and book chapters. In addition, John Kirk authored *Healthcare without Borders: Understanding Cuban Medical Internationalism* (2015), William LeoGrande coauthored *Back Channel to Cuba: The Hidden History of Negotiations between Washington and Havana* (2015), and Philip Brenner coauthored *Cuba Libre: A 500-Year Quest for Independence* (2018). Two of us were in Havana in December 2014, when Presidents Castro and Obama announced that their countries would restore diplomatic relations, and we experienced Cubans' palpable exhilaration because it seemed that the yoke of a fifty-five-year conflict had been lifted from their backs. We also felt the disappointment colleagues and friends shared upon learning that the final draft of the new constitution did not include a provision in the earlier draft that had defined marriage as "the voluntary union of two legally qualified persons in order to live together in common" without any specification of gender.

Our awareness about Cuba's circumstances convinced us that it was too soon for a third edition of the *Reader*, because too much was changing too rapidly. Yet we also wanted readers—students, visitors, and an informed public curious about this extraordinary country—to have an accessible book that helps them understand what happened in Cuba in the recent past and what is occurring today, and to appreciate why the country finds itself at a crossroads: a point at which the decisions it makes now about its sources of productive growth, food and energy, the relationship between the state and its citizens, and the way it manages its relations with other countries will determine whether Cuba succeeds in revitalizing its revolution.

In "Introduction: An Overview of Cuba from 2006 to 2019," Philip Brenner provides the context for the subsequent chapters by reviewing the twelve years of Raúl Castro's presidency and the first year of Miguel Díaz-Canel's national leadership. William LeoGrande's "Politics: The Challenges Facing Cuba's New Leaders" focuses on political changes occurring from 2014 to 2019 and highlights the significance of both the peaceful transition of power and key provisions in the new constitution. In chapter 2, "Cuba's Economy: Reforms and Delays, 2014–2018," Ricardo Torres describes the several ways in which Cuba has attempted to modernize the economy since 2014, and he analyzes the key factors that have contributed to the economy's current stagnation. John Kirk's chapter, "Cuban Foreign Policy, 2014–2019: From Raúl Castro to Miguel Díaz-Canel," details the way in which a changing international landscape has transformed a context that seemed pregnant with positive possibilities into one fraught with challenges, and he highlights the changes and continuities in Cuba's foreign policy. In chapter 4, "Cuban Society: Becoming More Unequal, Connected, and Diverse," Katrin Hansing and Bert Hoffmann explore how the economic changes since 2014 and the introduction of new technology have created fresh opportunities for entrepreneurs and an explosion of new films, music, art, and literature while at the same time increasing inequality and racial disparities that are an obstacle to achieving equity.

Cuba at the Crossroads includes a chronology from 2014 to 2019, a list of useful websites for further exploration of the country, and a set of excerpts from primary documents that highlight key decisions and new structures. The editors appreciate the assistance of Teresa García Castro and Elisabeth Hutcheson in compiling the chronology.

This book would not have been possible without the willingness of Cuban officials to engage with us, several Cuban institutions to open their doors for us, and Cuban colleagues and friends to share their insights and experiences with us, for which we are grateful. Jina Shim, an MA student at American University, deserves special acknowledgment for her careful and intelligent construction of the book's index. We also appreciate the encouragement and support that Susan McEachern and Katelyn Turner at Rowman & Littlefield have provided. Above all, our families continue to be a source of energy and inspiration for us.

Philip Brenner
John M. Kirk
William M. LeoGrande
January 2020

Introduction

An Overview of Cuba from 2006 to 2019

Philip Brenner

On July 31, 2006, a gravely ill Fidel Castro handed his conductor's baton to Raúl Castro. When the younger brother of Cuba's larger-than-life revolutionary leader accepted the provisional reins of power as head of state and commander-in-chief of the Revolutionary Armed Forces, a new era began in Cuba.[1]

It was the moment about which US policymakers and many Cuban exiles had been dreaming, when they thought chaos would ensue and the revolutionary regime would collapse. Fearing its wishes might come true in the form of a massive exodus, the George W. Bush administration warned Cubans "against leaving the island."[2] But there was no turmoil, no rush for the exit. The transition occurred almost seamlessly. Historian Julia Sweig aptly characterized the handover as the Cuban leader's "final victory."[3]

Fidel Castro had been the indispensable person without whom the Cuban Revolution would have taken a different course. Yet he was not a traditional Latin American caudillo. From 1959 to 2006, the country's economy, politics, foreign policy, culture, and social organization were not merely a reflection of Castro's personality and personal predilections because the Cuban Revolution had an organic quality. It grew from below and was shaped by the relationship between leader and followers. As sociologist Nelson Valdés explains, Castro was a *charismatic* leader. "His charismatic authority would not have been possible without the revolutionary practices which the Cuban populace embraced."[4]

For a government to remain legitimate after the passing of its charismatic leader, it needs to substitute one of two other forms of legitimacy, which sociologist Max Weber termed traditional and legal-institutional.[5] Consider

that the US federal government at first relied on George Washington's charismatic leadership for its legitimacy and then turned to tradition. Succeeding
presidents through John Quincy Adams endowed the new government with
legitimacy by their ties to the American Revolution. However, fifty-three
years after the start of the Independence War, the revolutionary heroes or
their sons were no longer available. President Andrew Jackson of Tennessee,
who took office in 1829, had been born outside one of the original thirteen
states and was only nine years old when the revolution began. He ushered in
a new era during which the right to vote was expanded significantly to male
non–property owners and contributed to the government's legal-institutional
legitimacy.[6]

Establishing governmental legitimacy was a primary task that confronted
Raúl Castro in 2006. Of course, as one of the Cuban Revolution's leaders, he
could rely on traditional authority. In addition, he did surround himself at
first with leaders whose right to rule derived from their personal participation
in the revolution. Still, Raúl was seventy-six years old, and his colleagues—
the "historic" generation that overthrew Fulgencio Batista in 1959—were of
the same vintage. High on his agenda was reinforcing the legal-institutional
authority that would be necessary to sustain the Cuban Revolution in the
future.[7] At the same time, he had to bring about change, to lead the country
toward a model appropriate for the twenty-first century that would enable it
to develop independently, maintain its commitment to providing basic needs
equally for all Cubans, and sustain Cuba's high standing in Latin America
and the Third World. This chapter provides an overview of how Cuba attempted to fulfill that agenda from 2006 to 2019. The chapters that follow fill
in the details of the story from 2014 to the first half of 2019.[8]

POLITICS AND ECONOMICS

A Profound Debate

By 2006, the Cuban government had weathered a "Special Period" of hardships caused by the cancellation of the Soviet Union's subsidies and aid, and
its ultimate dissolution. Cuba's resulting 29 percent decline in Gross Domestic Product might have destabilized most other countries. Still it was clear
that political and economic reforms were necessary if the Cuban Revolution
was going to be sustainable. The Cuban people had demonstrated a remarkable resilience and ability to adapt, but the new leader could not be certain
how much longer they would be patient. Recognizing that his authority was
tenuous, Raúl proceeded cautiously. He quoted Fidel in every speech, wrap-
ping himself in his brother's authority, and made no dramatic moves during
his first eighteen months in office. Yet he also began to prepare the country
for what he hoped would be a reinvented Cuban Revolution.

An October 2006 investigative report on corruption in *Juventud Rebelde*, the official newspaper of the Communist Party's youth wing, was an early signal of changes to come. Headlined "The Big Old Swindle," the series could not have appeared without Raúl's approval. It revealed what most people already suspected: state-owned stores routinely sold products that weighed less than the amount customers had paid for; food at state restaurants had less meat or cheese than regulations required.[9]

Two months later the acting president encouraged university students to engage in the kind of open debate about Cuba's future that his older brother had eschewed. The younger Castro asserted, "The first principle in constructing any armed forces is the sole command. But that doesn't mean that we cannot discuss . . . that way we reach decisions, and I'm talking about big decisions."[10]

He followed this admonition in July 2007 by offering a frank assessment of Cuba's economic circumstances in the annual address commemorating the 1953 *Moncada* attack. Raúl emphasized that the US embargo was only one of several external factors Cuba had to take into account in "ensuring the socialist principle that each should contribute according to their capacity and receive according to their work." The main issue, he declared, was that "No one, no individual or country, can afford to spend more than what they have. . . . To have more, we have to begin by producing more, with a sense of rationality and efficiency, so that we may reduce imports, especially of food products." Then he warned that to achieve this goal "structural and conceptual changes will have to be introduced."[11]

Members of the Communist Party and Young Communists studied the speech in detail over the next months, not as commandments to be repeated by rote, but as pronouncements to be debated and interpreted. Journalist Marc Frank obtained the guide prepared for discussion leaders and reports that it admonished them to foster a "profound debate." The main topics suggested for discussion included food production, import substitution, and increasing production and efficiency.[12]

However, as discussions moved beyond the Communist Party into work centers, community meetings, and even some publications, a new set of issues replaced the recommended topics. Cubans vented their anger over the dual currency system and their declining ability to purchase necessities with the state salaries they earned. Many complained about bureaucratic red tape, which made bribes an increasingly necessary cost in order to obtain a state service or license or to avoid trouble from inspectors or the police.[13]

There were still many achievements for which Cubans could be proud. The UN's 2009 *Human Development Report* ranked Cuba 51 out of 194 countries, just behind Argentina (49) and Uruguay (50), and ahead of Mexico (53), Costa Rica (54), and Brazil (75).[14] However, the Special Period clearly had taken an enormous toll. Increasing inequality, decreasing access to health care and a good education, and a growing culture of individualism and a declining sense of communal solidarity had eroded distinctive aspects of the Cuban Revolution. The wellspring of hope that nurtured Cubans' belief in the future, which had given them the energy and strength to defy the odds in building a new society, seemed depleted.

A Preference for Organizational Order

The 1976 constitution (and subsequent amended versions through 2002) proclaimed that the Cuban Communist Party (PCC) was "the highest leading force [*la fuerza dirigente superior*] of the society and State." Yet by 2008, the PCC was languishing. Led by old men and increasingly disconnected from the travails most Cubans felt, it had not held a party congress since 1997, though one was supposed to be organized every five years. In part, its decline resulted from Fidel's efforts to energize Cubans through participation in mass organizations disconnected from the PCC, such as the revitalized Federation of University Students, which he hoped would instill revolutionary fervor among younger Cubans. He also inaugurated several projects outside of regular institutional boundaries. Starting in 2000 and 2001, the government sent tens of thousands of youth whom it identified as "disaffected" to new schools of social work, where they were trained in a one-year course and then deployed to communities to work with the elderly, young prisoners, and the physically challenged. High-school students from eastern provinces went to Havana to teach in elementary schools abandoned by seasoned instructors who sought to earn hard currency in tourism or abroad. As an accompaniment to new projects, the government began to air university-level classes on television to train the "emergency teachers" and to provide new skills for laid-off workers in the downsized sugar industry. [15]

Most of these *ad hoc* efforts ended after the National Assembly formally elected Raúl as the new president in February 2008. In his inauguration speech, he emphasized the importance of institutionalization and reestablishing the role that the constitution had given to the PCC as the highest leading force of the society and state. "Fidel is Fidel, we all know it well. Fidel is irreplaceable," he declared, in effect acknowledging that this was the moment to transfer the basis of the revolution's legitimacy from charisma to legal-rational structures. "Only the Communist Party, the certain guarantor of the Cuban nation's unity," he declared, "can be the worthy heir to the confidence the people endow in their leader." [16] In contrast to his brother, Raúl had a decided preference for organizational order. He honored well-defined lines of authority and sought to establish accountability for achievements and errors.

Under Fidel's leadership, three power centers had overlapping authority: governmental ministries, the PCC, and the so-called Grupo de Apoyo (Support Group)—Fidel Castro's tight-knit, little-publicized kitchen cabinet of confidants who were in their twenties and early thirties. This arrangement not only led to duplication of efforts and poor coordination. It also allowed the people in each group to avoid taking responsibility for failures—passing the blame on to those in another group. With Fidel at the hub of the three-pronged power structure, stagnation tended to accompany any policy initiative. No one felt secure in making decisions; it seemed as if every action had to wait for the *comandante*'s approval. Even his closest allies acknowledged that Fidel could only make so many decisions that were based on well-reasoned analysis. Raúl would not run a system that he perceived was so chaotic.

The new president waited one year to institute any major reform. Then, in a quick stroke on March 2, 2009, he dismissed Carlos Lage Dávila, secretary of the Council of Ministers and vice president in charge of the Cuban economy; Fernando Remírez de Estenoz, head of the international committee of the Communist Party's Central Committee who had been a vice minister of foreign relations, ambassador to the United Nations, and head of the Cuban Interests Section in Washington; and eight ministers, including Foreign Minister Felipe Pérez Roque.

Lage, Remírez, and Pérez Roque had been members of Fidel's Grupo de Apoyo and were generally viewed as likely leaders among the generation that would take over when the *históricos* retired. The purge was less an attempt to put his own loyalists in place than it was to break down the competing lines of authority and establish the orderly administrative process he promised in his inaugural address. At the same time, Raúl combined four existing ministries into two (the Ministries of Foreign Trade and Investment and Food), and he promoted some younger PCC leaders whom he viewed as exemplary managers into key governmental positions. Most notable was Miguel Díaz-Canel Bermúdez, the Holguín Province party chief, who became minister of higher education and first vice president in 2013. The National Assembly elected him as Cuba's president in 2018.

Díaz-Canel had a reputation for being an efficient manager. Born in 1960, he studied to be an electronics engineer, spent three years in the army, and then rose in the Communist Party hierarchy. As PCC first secretary in the provinces of Villa Clara and Holguin, he also was known for fighting corruption, and soon after becoming president, he launched a campaign against corruption, calling it "the principal enemy of the revolution."[17]

Elected in 2016 to a five-year term, Raúl Castro continued as first secretary of the PCC in 2018. It was the first time since the founding of the modern PCC in 1965 that the president of the country and the PCC head were different people. Díaz-Canel tried to allay concerns that the division of power would be unmanageable, declaring in his first speech as president that he would "be faithful to Fidel and Raúl," adding that Raúl "will take the lead on decisions of greatest importance for the present and future of the country."[18] Six weeks later the National Assembly named Raúl to head a commission to draft a new Cuban constitution.

2019 Constitution

Raúl provided the official rationale for drafting a new constitution in 2016, telling the Seventh Party Congress that it was needed as a response to "historical circumstances, and social and economic conditions, which have changed with the passing of time."[19] Yet the most significant political changes in the new constitution—which voters approved by a wide margin in a February 2019 referendum—potentially reduce some of the president's power and decentralize some authority to local governments. For example, the Council of State is now headed by the president of the National Assembly, not the president of the country. All of the council's members are elected deputies in the National Assembly, which meets only twice each year in short sessions. When it is not in session, the Council of State issues decrees on the legislature's behalf. Given this new structure in which the heads of the legislative and executive branches are different people, it is notable that 58 percent of the deputies whom voters elected in 2018 had not served previously in the National Assembly. Also, for the first time, its membership closely reflected the gender (48.4 percent women) and racial (41 percent black and mixed race) composition of the country.[20]

The constitution also guarantees political rights not in the previous one. These include habeas corpus and the right to be presumed innocent in trials and to be free from torture and inhumane treatment or punishment. It also contains provisions on religious freedom and declares all "people are equal before the law," regardless of sex, gender, gender identity, sexual orientation, skin color, age, religious beliefs, or ethnicity. With 229 articles, the 2019 constitution sets out an ambitious agenda of change, and most of the provisions require follow-up legislation and regulation for implementation. As Geoff Thale and Teresa García Castro observe, "That process is likely to be gradual and complicated."[21] This is especially true of the several articles in the constitution intended to update the Cuban economy.

Slowly Updating the Cuban Economy

The changes in Cuba's political structure after 2006 were accompanied by only minor economic reforms at first. In July 2007, the government announced it would lease fallow land to private farmers, reduce restrictions on the free market sales of produce, and raise the prices it paid to farmers for produce. (These plans were set back over the next two months as Hurricanes Gustav and Ike left 200,000 Cubans homeless, and destroyed 25,900 metric tons of agricultural crops, including 50 percent of the sugar crop, 90 percent of the tobacco crop, and 80 percent of the plantain and banana crop.) In 2007 and 2008, the government also began to issue licenses that allowed drivers to use private cars as taxis, and it lifted the ban on selling computers, DVD players, and cell phones and permitted Cubans to pay for services—such as hotel rooms, food in tourist hotels, or rental cars—with Cuban convertible currency.

Economist Jorge Mario Sánchez aptly observed that the economic changes "pointed in the right direction but were insufficient to deal with the roots of dysfunctionality."[22] Cuba still had not found a way to generate enough hard currency to develop a sustainable and equitable economy. While its gross domestic product had reached $100 billion, hard currency earnings amounted to only 4 percent of the total. The country continued to spend too much on importing food that it could have grown domestically.[23]

In response, Raúl set off an economic shock in April 2010. Charging that "the budgeted and entrepreneurial sectors have hundreds of thousands of workers in excess," he announced a plan to reduce the size of the state's workforce by one million employees—a cut of nearly 20 percent.[24] Several problems had combined to lead to this one solution. The government was strapped for cash to pay workers. Some laid-off state workers, officials reasoned, might accept the government's offer of up to forty hectares (about one hundred acres) of free land on which they could increase domestic food production. Raúl also believed that government workers treated their jobs as sinecures—guaranteed regardless of what they did—which encouraged sloth resulting low productivity.

As one might readily guess, popular reaction to the speech was negative, and resistance to the plan emerged from within the government as well. In August 2010, the president revised his numbers. He said that the reduction would be more moderate—the state would drop only five hundred thousand from its payroll, with much of the decrease occurring through retirement and attrition. Nevertheless, he was adamant that change had to come. "We must erase forever the notion that Cuba is the only country in the world where one can live without working," he told the National Assembly.[25] Moreover, he pressed senior officials to quicken the pace of change, a process he labeled as "updating the Cuban economy."

Privatization

In November 2010, "updating" was formalized as a major new program of economic revitalization, "Guidelines of the Economic and Social Policy of the Party and the Revolution," known as *Lineamientos* or Guidelines.[26] It outlined 291 proposals for reform, which became 313 after widespread public discussions in work centers, community meetings, mass organizations, and schools. Only 32 percent of the original 291 guidelines remained unmod-

ified. Some were combined with others, and an additional thirty-six guidelines emerged from the nationwide series of meetings.[27] The 313 *Lineamientos* established a process for expanding the number of permissible private
(referred to as "non-state") sector enterprises. It created a commission that
initially listed 181 types of private occupations that could be performed
legally. Within two years, the commission added more than fifty other categories. The list included mostly service jobs, such as barber or beautician,
electrician, bricklayer, plumber, photographer, waiter, truck driver, flower
seller, entertainer, sports instructor, and so on.[28] The Sixth Party Congress
approved the plan in April 2011.

Cuban economist Juan Triana explained that the *Lineamientos* provided a
fundamentally new orientation for the society. The "consensus that without
development it will be very hard to sustain Cuban socialism," he wrote, "is a
departure from the past in which socialism was the guarantor of achieving
development."[29] Notably, Cuba's leaders acknowledged that development
might need to prioritize efficiency and growth, which would require a greater
reliance on market factors in determining wages and even what enterprises
produced.[30]

The Seventh Party Congress revised the *Lineamientos* in 2016 and approved two additional documents as a basis for further reform: "Conceptualization of the Cuban Social and Economic Model of Socialist Development"
and the "National Plan of Economic and Social Development to 2030."
While maintaining aspirations of equity and full employment, the new plans
made clear that the non-state sector would be a permanent feature of Cuba's
economy. The 2019 constitution affirmed this by recognizing private ownership of productive as well as personal property (Article 22), and guaranteeing
that foreign investment is an "important element for the economic development of the country" (Article 28).

In 2011, at about the same time that the PCC approved the original *Lineamientos*, the government eased several regulations related to small businesses. *Paladares*—private restaurants in homes—were permitted to employ
nonfamily members as workers, and the limit on the number of patrons a
paladar could serve at one time was raised at first from twelve to fifty diners
and later was effectively scrapped when restaurateurs were allowed to own
multiple licenses for the same establishment. In 2018, as inequality grew and
some entrepreneurs were becoming millionaires, the government ruled that a
family could own only one *paladar*. Pushback from entrepreneurs led officials to withdraw the regulation.

Bed-and-breakfast accommodations in the 1990s and early 2000s had
been confined to rooms within a dwelling occupied by the vendor. A modified rule allowed an entrepreneur to rent out a whole apartment or house—
which became the most popular option for Airbnb participants when the
company entered Cuba in 2015. Late in 2011, the government decreed that

individuals could buy and sell houses and automobiles directly to one another for the first time in fifty years.

The *Lineamientos* and the new constitution roughly indicate the nature and extent of privatization that Cuba's leaders envisioned for the country: between 40 and 50 percent of Cuba's workers would be employed in non-state sector jobs; major resources—nickel mines, oil fields, energy production—would continue to be state-owned; the state would maintain near exclusive monopoly to provide education, day care, and health care.

Slightly more than 75 percent of Cuba's population lived in urban areas in 2009.[31] While the plan to increase food production by enticing city dwellers to rural areas with the offer of free land began that year, there were few takers. Aside from the expectation that the work would be difficult, the incentives were low and the hurdles were high. A family's rights over improvements to the land—such as a barn—remained unclear. Moreover, as political geographer Garrett Graddy-Lovelace reports, there was a "thirty percent rate of food loss from field to store" in 2015 because farmers often lacked "bags, bushels, crates, and boxes to transport harvested crops."[32]

In 2012 and 2013, the government partially responded to the problems by easing and clarifying some regulations, especially for cooperatives. The area of land a cooperative could lease was increased to sixty-seven hectares (about 165 acres), and leases could extend to twenty-five years instead of ten. Cooperatives also were permitted to sell directly to hotels and other tourism entities instead of going through a state entity. Both cooperatives and individual farmers were allowed to retain the right to the structures they had built on the land.[33]

Meanwhile, through its urban and suburban farm programs, Cuba continued to promote agroecology, emphasizing a minimum use of fossil fuels and locating producers close to consumers. Suburban farmers, though, faced obstacles that are uncommon for urban farmers. Plots in the suburbs are larger, which makes maintenance solely with human labor impossible. Transporting produce to cities also is more difficult to sustain without the use of fossil fuels for trucks. To overcome these hurdles, suburban farmers relied on animal power—oxen teams—and the Agriculture Ministry set up collection stations to which farmers can travel by carts to deposit their produce.[34]

Running in Place

One bright glimmer on the horizon in 2006 had faded by 2013. Preliminary geological surveys showed that Cuba had significant oil reserves offshore in the Florida Straits, ranging between 4.6 and 20 billion barrels.[35] But extracting the petroleum, which was in deep undersea deposits, was so costly that foreign investors would not be able to recover the expense until the price of oil reached at least $125/barrel, which was becoming less likely in the near future. The possibility that oil would save the Cuban Revolution was, at best, many years away.

As a result, even though small businesses were flourishing when the Cuban Communist Party held its Seventh Congress in 2016, many Cubans complained that all of their bustling still left them only running in place, that Raúl was implementing changes too slowly. Indeed, he acknowledged in mid-2016 that the Cuban economy was suffering severe problems and warned that it would be "imperative to reduce expenses of all kinds that are not indispensable, to promote a culture of conservation and the efficient use of resources available."[36] Similarly, the PCC Congress reported that only 21 percent of the reforms intended to "update" the Cuban economic model had been fulfilled completely.[37]

Two significant problems stood in the path of updating the economy. First, Cuba had no other country's blueprint to follow; no country had been able to achieve its twin goals of development with equity and independence. Second, opponents of reform were scattered throughout the government and PCC, especially at key decision points. Some were self-serving survivalists who had found ways to adapt to hardship through informal networks and illegal practices that economic reforms would disturb. Others sincerely worried that foreign investments could make Cuba vulnerable to the demands of another country and vitiate Cuba's sovereignty, or that Cuba's unfettered integration into the global economy would lead Cubans to replace values of social responsibility and communal cooperation with extreme individualism and consumerism.

The situation of nonagricultural cooperatives illustrates how opponents of change could slow down the process. A municipal agency was able to approve a license for an individual private business (*cuentapropista*). Yet only the Council of Ministers could authorize the operation of a nonagricultural cooperative. As a result, there were only 450 of these cooperatives functioning in mid-2018, most of which were spun off from state enterprises located in Havana. At the same time, few licenses had been issued for private professional activities—legal representation, architecture, business consulting, accounting—even though post-2011 regulations permitted such professionals to form cooperatives.

In 2016, the economy experienced two consecutive quarters of negative growth (i.e., a recession) for the first time in nearly a quarter century. The next year GDP growth was an anemic 1.2 and only 1.8 percent in 2018. As Ricardo Torres elaborates in his chapter in this book, this is "well below the needs of a country the size and level of development of Cuba" and is incompatible "with a sustained improvement in the living conditions of a majority of Cubans." Moreover, a drop of foreign currency earnings in late 2018 and early 2019 resulted in a shortage of products of all kinds. In May 2019, the

Ministry of Internal Commerce announced the rationing of chicken, eggs, rice, beans, and several hygienic products such as soap.

The tourism sector was the only leading export with robust performance and continues to be one of the pillars of Cuba's economy. Tourist arrivals jumped from 2.2 million in 2006 to 4.75 million in 2018. The total included 638,000 non–Cuban American US travelers, a 22 percent increase over 2016. But in June 2019, US president Donald Trump ended "people-to-people" educational travel—a license category that enabled most of the 638,000 to visit Cuba legally—and banned US cruise vessels from docking in Cuba.[38]

FOREIGN RELATIONS

As Raúl Castro took over the reins of leadership in 2006, Cuba was at a high point in its relations with countries in Latin America, Africa, and Asia, and at a nadir in its relations with the United States and Europe. In December 2006, Cuba hosted the summit of the Nonaligned Movement (NAM) for the second time and became chair for the next three years. (Only Yugoslavia, another founding member of the NAM, had been honored to host the summit twice.) By the end of its three-year term as NAM chair, all of the countries in the Western Hemisphere except the United States had established diplomatic relations with Cuba. In November 2008, Cuba also became a full member of the Rio Group, an informal association of twenty-three Western Hemispheric countries that formalized itself in 2011 as the Community of Latin American and Caribbean States (CELAC in the Spanish acronym) and seemed to offer a potential challenge to the OAS (Organization of American States) as the main forum for handling hemispheric issues.

Continuity from Fidel to Raúl

No one expected Raúl to shift Cuba's foreign policy from the internationalist path it had taken under Fidel. After all, the new leader had been vice president and minister of the armed forces for more than forty years and was a partner with his brother in establishing the path. Still, there were changes occasioned by new opportunities and challenges in the international landscape.

By 2007, China had become Cuba's second-largest trading partner, after Venezuela, with $2.3 billion in bilateral trade that year. When Chinese president Hu Jintao visited Cuba the following year, he approved a $6 billion investment for the expansion of a Cienfuegos oil refinery and the construction of a liquefied natural gas plant, and provided the second phase of a $350 million loan designated for the renovation of Cuban hospitals.[39] On the heels of President Hu's visit, Russian president Dmitri Medvedev came to Cuba to sign trade agreements involving nickel, oil, automobiles, and wheat.

Still, Latin America was the region that offered the greatest promise for Cuba. Nearly every Latin American country had experienced meaningful economic growth between 1990 and 2010. Brazil's GDP grew by more than 40 percent, and it moved from eleventh to seventh place in the world's ranking. Cuba reached out to Brazil partly as a way of diversifying its trading partners, and it established a joint venture with Odebrecht, the Brazilian engineering conglomerate, to reconstruct the Port of Mariel at a cost of $1 billion. The port opened in January 2014 with a terminal that has an annual capacity of one million containers and the ability to service super cargo ships traversing the recently widened Panama Canal.

Significantly, Brazil's growth was inclusive, bringing many more people into the middle class than ever before, which was also the situation in several other countries in the region that had reduced inequality and poverty and expanded their middle class. These changes did not result from the "magic" of the free market or reduced government spending as preached by Washington. Well-planned government programs, such as the Bolsa Familia subsidy in Brazil, brought about the improvements. Indeed, the leftward shift in Latin America brought to power in the first decade of the twenty-first century several leaders who had long admired Cuba. This was one reason they selected Cuba to host the second CELAC summit, which convened in January 2014 in Havana.

Until at least 2013, the most important institution that helped to strengthen Cuba's bilateral relations in the region was the Bolivarian Alliance for the Peoples of Our America (ALBA in the Spanish acronym). Venezuelan president Hugo Chávez put forward in 2001 the idea of integrating the hemisphere via ALBA, and it began operations in 2004, backed by Venezuela's oil wealth.

In conjunction with ALBA, Cuba provided medical aid—including a program to restore eyesight to more than two million people—in several Latin American and Caribbean countries beginning in 2005.[40] That year as well, the Latin American School of Medicine (ELAM in the Spanish acronym) graduated its first class of doctors. A tuition-free institution in Havana, ELAM was created to train students from underserved populations in Africa, Asia, and the Western Hemisphere, including the United States. John Kirk explains that Cuba's "tradition of medical internationalism dates back to 1960." As of 2011, the international medical program was sending about 41,000 health workers to sixty-eight nations.[41]

While the commitment to medical internationalism continued apace under Raúl, despite setbacks in the domestic economy, it also became an important way for Cuba to earn hard currency—as Cuba charged fees to countries that could afford them—and increase the wages of Cuban doctors. The services they provided in Brazil, Bolivia, Venezuela, and Ecuador brought medical care to rural communities and urban pockets of poverty that had never seen a doctor. In turn, it strengthened popular support for the leaders in those countries, which reinforced their inclination to support Cuba.

Also meeting in Havana at the time of the CELAC summit were peace negotiators from the Colombian government and the Revolutionary Armed Forces of Colombia (FARC), the main insurgent group in the country. The peace negotiations began in mid-November 2012 in Norway and quickly moved to Havana, where Cuban diplomats played a critical role in helping to bring about an agreement four years later.

However, by 2019 circumstances in Latin America had changed in ways that were less favorable to Cuba. Between 2013 and 2019, Venezuela's economy declined significantly due to a drop in world oil prices, corruption, the government's failure to maintain the petroleum industry's infrastructure, the out-migration of technical experts, and international sanctions. It was no longer able to provide the same level of subsidies to Cuba or to support ALBA. Corruption also led to the downfall of Brazilian governments that had good relations with Cuba. In 2018, Brazilian president-elect Jair Bolsonaro effectively ended the program of Cuban medical assistance by demanding doctors meet untenable conditions, which removed eight thousand doctors from underserved Brazilian areas—with a loss to Cuba of several hundred million dollars. Elections in Chile, Peru, and Colombia also brought arch-conservatives to power who sought to gain favor with the United States by distancing their countries from Cuba.

Slow Opening with the United States

Colombia had been the third-largest recipient of US economic and military aid in the world—an average of more than $700 million per year for over two decades. Thus, Colombian president Juan Manuel Santos's stark ultimatum at the end of the 2012 Summit of the Americas shocked US officials. Speaking on behalf of the other heads of state, he declared they would not attend the summit planned for 2015 unless Cuba was permitted to participate.[42] Back in Washington, President Barack Obama fired his national security advisor for Latin America, and then, shortly after his November reelection, decided to pursue normal diplomatic relations with Cuba. In April 2013, he assigned two top aides to begin negotiations toward that goal.[43]

Cuba had bought a record $711 million worth of food, agricultural equipment, and medicine from the United States in 2008. Despite the embargo, the hovering giant had become the island's fifth-largest trading partner.[44] Some Cuban officials hoped that the purchases would encourage major US companies to lobby for a changed US policy, but the Obama administration's policy during his first term disappointed them.

During the 2008 presidential campaign, Senator Obama said he would be willing to meet with President Castro, and he took office as president with little obligation to Cuban American hard-liners. His margin of victory in Florida—204,600 votes—was large enough that he virtually did not need any Cuban American votes to win the state, though approximately 35 percent of their ballots were cast for him.[45] He also had political cover created by a flurry of proposals for better relations from several ad hoc groups made up of former US government officials and members of Congress, leading scholars, and prominent public intellectuals, several of whom had previously supported harsh measures against Cuba.[46] This context provided enough political space for President Obama to fulfill a campaign promise by removing restrictions on remittances sent by Cuban Americans. He also reversed President Bush's restrictive travel policy for Cuban Americans. In 2011, President Obama increased the level of remittances all US citizens could send to Cuba and eased some restrictions on educational travel. Moreover, the administration restarted semi-annual migration talks with Cuba and increased diplomatic contacts at a slightly higher level than before.

From the Cuban perspective, the administration's actions were too modest, because they did little to reduce economic sanctions under the US embargo and the Obama administration had made no move to remove Cuba from the US State Department's list of state sponsors of terrorism. Meanwhile, Washington continued several programs that Cuba perceived as harmful or threatening.

One project, the Cuban Medical Professional Parole (CMPP) program created in 2006, was designed to encourage Cuban doctors serving abroad to give up their citizenship and immigrate to the United States. By the end of 2015, the United States had approved more than seven thousand applications from Cuban medical personnel.[47] The US Agency for International Development (USAID) was the lead agency in spending funds on covert programs that Cuba considered subversive. In 2009, it spent $45 million on these projects.[48] The one that created the greatest obstacle for improved relations involved Alan P. Gross, a subcontractor for Development Alternatives International. The Cuban government arrested Gross in December 2009 and asserted that his mission was "to establish illegal and covert communications systems . . . intended to destabilize the existing order."[49] The State Department claimed he was in Cuba merely to provide the small Jewish community with telecommunications equipment that would enable its members to access the internet without Cuban government interference or surveillance. The Jewish community had not requested such assistance.

In fact, what Gross provided was sophisticated satellite communications transmitters that included a subscriber identity module (SIM) card usually available only to the US military or intelligence community. The SIM card could prevent the detection of signals from the transmitters for a radius of 250 miles.[50] The communications setup Gross established would allow a Cuban enemy to communicate with its operatives inside Cuba, or allow subversive groups to communicate across the island by tapping into the equipment that Gross had given to Jewish communities in three Cuban cities and was planning to distribute more widely.

Following Gross's arrest, the State Department ended the renewed migration talks and refused to consider offers by Cuban representatives to discuss a variety of bilateral issues. (However, US and Cuban officials continued monthly meetings at the Guantánamo Naval Base fence line and maintained cooperation over drug enforcement.)[51] Judging that the Obama administration was unlikely to make any major move to improve relations, the Cuban government cut back its purchases of US exports to $533 million in 2009.

Several events and circumstances in 2013 offered renewed expectations for improved relations. A new Cuban law enabled most citizens to obtain passports, to leave the country for up to two years without an exit permit, and to return without forfeiting their property. The United States previously had highlighted Cuba's travel restrictions in attacking its human rights record.[52]

The month after the 2013 negotiations on normalization began, a federal judge—with the concurrence of the Justice Department—permitted René González, one of the Cuban Five, to stay in Cuba permanently after he was allowed to travel there to attend memorial services for his father. He had been released on parole in 2011 after thirteen years in prison but was forced to serve out his parole in the United States. In November 2013, President Obama hinted at big changes. "Keep in mind that when Castro came to power, I was just born," he said at a fundraiser. "So the notion that the same policies that we put in place in 1961 would somehow still be as effective as they are today . . . doesn't make sense."[53]

Obama Opens the Door and Trump Closes It

On December 17, 2014, Presidents Castro and Obama revealed what had been in the works for the previous eighteen months, announcing that their countries would resume diplomatic relations. President Castro also announced Cuba had released Gross, the USAID subcontractor, on humanitarian grounds and would also release fifty-three political prisoners. President Obama said that he had commuted the sentences of the three remaining members of the Cuban Five still in prison and returned them to Cuba. Cuba did the same for a CIA agent arrested in the 1990s. President Obama also indicated he would consider removing Cuba from the US list of state sponsors of terrorism. (He did so in May 2015.)

As the two governments sought to make the movement toward normal relations "irreversible" in 2015 and 2016, they engaged in a flurry of activity and produced almost two dozen agreements. Negotiations cut across a range of issues, including environmental cooperation, law enforcement, combating trafficking in persons, and property claims. Regularly scheduled airline service, direct postal services, advanced telecommunications connections, and new avenues for commerce were made possible when the United States relaxed some sanctions and the State Department removed Cuba from its list of state sponsors of terrorism. One notable agreement led to new Treasury Department rules that allow US citizens to engage in joint medical research projects with Cuban nationals and permit the importation of Cuban-origin pharmaceuticals. This enabled the Roswell Park Cancer Institute in Buffalo, New York, to begin clinical trials on CIMAvax, a Cuban drug that may pave the way to developing a lung cancer vaccine. In March 2016, President Obama even traveled to Havana with his family and a large contingent of US senators and representatives.

Republican presidential candidate Donald Trump asserted correctly that as president he would have the authority to reverse nearly all of President Obama's initiatives, because they had been achieved through executive orders, not legislation. Yet by mid-2017 he reversed only one of the sanctions President Obama had relaxed, requiring that US citizens travel to Cuba for educational purposes only with a licensed travel provider. He also added a new sanction that banned any commerce with a Cuban entity owned or controlled by the military, which placed many hotels, restaurants, and stores off-limits to Americans.

Far more significant was the State Department's decision to label a series of illnesses experienced by twenty-four US embassy personnel as "sonic attacks," for which it asserted Cuba should bear responsibility. The illnesses, which in the most severe cases mimicked the kind of concussion that occurs from a physical blow to the head, occurred over a period of several months in late 2016 and 2017. A study published in the *Journal of the American Medical Association* reported that three or four people in the group had persistent cognitive, balance, auditory, or visual impairment more than three months after initially experiencing a problem.[54] Yet, as a May 2019 *New York Times* article reported, "the claims of an attack by an invisible weapon remain not only unproved but also highly contested by prominent physicists and engineers in the United States and abroad."[55]

Despite the uncertainty about the cause of the problems, and with no evidence that Cuba had caused or had taken insufficient action to prevent the harm, the Trump administration evacuated most of the embassy staff from the country and designated Cuba as an unaccompanied post. It then demanded that Cuba reduce the size of its embassy staff in Washington and issued a travel warning about Cuba. The consequences were that several US organizations canceled planned educational trips to the island, and Cubans seeking a visa for travel to the United States had to travel to a third country to obtain one.

In November 2018, US national security advisor John Bolton launched a new series of attacks on Cuba that brought relations close to their most contentious since the end of the Cold War. He announced there would be additional sanctions and characterized Cuba as one of three countries in a "troika of tyranny." In April 2019, Secretary of State Mike Pompeo announced that President Trump would not waive Title III of the 1996 Cuban Liberty and Democratic Solidarity (Libertad) Act, also known as the Helms-Burton Act, despite opposition from US allies. Title III permits US citizens to sue in a US court any corporation or individual allegedly "trafficking" in property of theirs expropriated by the Cuban government, even if the persons had not been US citizens at the time of the expropriation. Two months later, the Trump administration canceled licenses for organizations taking Americans on "people-to-people" educational trips, capped at $1,000 every three months the previously unlimited amount of remittances Americans could send to their Cuban families, and, as noted previously, banned US cruise vessels from docking in Cuba.

Soft Power

"Soft power" is a term that connotes the ability of a country to influence others by example rather than by coercion. Cuba had accumulated its soft power through several mechanisms by the time Raúl became president. In addition to international medical and cooperative aid programs, these included: appealing to other Third World countries as an underdog who resists US oppression; supporting solidarity groups throughout the world; focusing on Cuba's own war against terrorism and its suffering from terrorism; and exporting Cuban films, music, and ballet. All have contributed to a positive image that enables Cuba "to be seen as a trusted and valued partner in many international arenas and institutions," despite its lack of Western liberal democracy, as historians Julia Sweig and Michael Bustamante observed.[56]

Cuba's soft power explains its success at the 2012 Summit of the Americas, despite being absent from the meeting. Its soft power in effect countered the hard power—military strength and financial levers—Washington traditionally used to dominate the hemisphere, when the United States backed down and agreed to allow Cuba to participate in future summits. Political scientist Tom Long describes such a case as "collective foreign policy," where a small country can influence a larger one because of its "ability to win international allies and to work with other small and medium states."[57]

In addition to medical internationalism, Cuba made itself a center for regional culture events with an arts festival (Havana Biennial) and annual jazz and film festivals, which attract tens of thousands of attendees. Sandra Levinson has noted that the "Havana Biennial has become a major showcase for 'Third World' art, an incredible accomplishment and commitment given Cuba's financial constraints."[58] Latin Americans accord the annual writing prizes from Casa de las Americas the level of prestige that the Pulitzer Prize has in the United States. Cuban music, films, and art—and, of course, Che Guevara T-shirts—are popular throughout the world. The global appreciation for Cuban culture took off during the Special Period when the government permitted artists and musicians to earn money abroad because it could no longer afford to support them. The internet subsequently gave them the possibility of getting worldwide exposure.

CULTURE AND SOCIAL RELATIONS

New Spaces for Expression

In 2012, Cuba's Ministry of Culture and the National Book Institute awarded the National Literature Prize to Leonardo Padura for *The Man Who Loved Dogs*. The decision to give Padura the country's most prestigious award for writing was, in effect, an open acceptance of dissent. All of Padura's detective novels had a political edge, exposing some form of corruption beneath the official façade of normalcy. *The Man Who Loved Dogs* is an epic work that weaves three stories into one. Each challenges an aspect of Cuba's politics, alleged ideological rigidity, or seemingly blind adherence to Soviet dogmas.

The shift toward greater freedom of expression actually began before Raúl became president. *Temas* magazine, for example, celebrated its twentieth anniversary in 2015. By publishing articles on topics rarely covered in the official media, and with views well outside the mainstream, the magazine helped to expand the borders of what was acceptable. Its July/September 2012 issue, for example, examined the subject of "Social Development," which included an article about the lack of social mobility and the transmission of poverty from one generation to the next.

Two magazines sponsored by the office of Cardinal Jaime Ortega y Alamino, the archbishop of Havana, also provided venues for open debate. *Palabra Nueva*, first published in 1992, and *Espacio Laical*, which started in 2005, included numerous articles about inequality in Cuba, the government's development strategy, and "the everyday life of the Cubans—the hopes, the expectations, their frustrations," as Orlando Márquez, *Palabra Nueva*'s longtime editor remarked in 2013.[59] For example, in an October 2011 article, *Espacio Laical* examined how the diaspora community could constructively become involved in developing the Cuban economy. In January 2013, it published a symposium that considered the need for a fundamental restructuring of the media in Cuba to broaden and democratize participation in decision-making.[60]

Temas's editor, Rafael Hernández, argues that increased access to digital media also accelerated the transformation of Cuba's civil culture, including mass cultural consumption and production.[61] By 2014, there had been a revival of periodicals and public spaces for debate on topics as diverse as the nature of socialist democracy, human rights, citizen participation, violence, local initiatives, urban and community problems, religious faiths, and gender.[62]

Still, Cuba lagged behind many other countries in providing access to the internet for several years. By the end of 2013 less than 5 percent of the population had full access.[63] In part, this was due to the US embargo, which prevented Cuba from using the services of US companies that dominated global connectivity and accessing the undersea fiber optic cables that literally surround the island. It was due, also, to technical problems in building a fiber optic cable connecting Cuba to Venezuela, which began operation only in January 2013. Ever resourceful, Cubans used an intranet network accessible on the island to communicate digitally. However, by 2017, the percentage of Cubans using the internet had risen to 57 percent.[64] Moreover, in December 2018 the Cuban government made internet access even more readily available by enabling Cubans to purchase 3G cell phone service.

In addition to cyber platforms, digital information is widely disseminated across the island through the *paquete semanal* (weekly package), a nonstate digital data distribution system. The *paquete* gathers thousands of hours of material from sources worldwide—mostly in violation of international copyright—from broadcast networks, distributors such as Netflix and Hulu, video game purveyors, and news and sports outlets. It then sells particular programs, entire seasons, or films to individuals who download them to a portable medium such as a USB drive.[65] Television shows that were available during the week of July 15, 2019, for example, included *Big Little Lies*, *The Big Bang Theory*, *Jimmy Kimmel Live*, *City on a Hill*, *Queen of the South*, and numerous international films.[66]

Until the Special Period, the Cuban Institute of Cinematographic Art and Industry (ICAIC) was the only distributor of Cuban films and provided most of the support for production. However, as filmmaking with limited resources grew ever more difficult, the government permitted filmmakers to search for funding outside of the country. Coproduction gave them the opportunity to explore subjects previously taboo in Cuba.[67] This was ever more apparent in the 2010 to 2013 period, with films such as *Revolución* (2010) on underground culture, *Habanastation* (2011) on inequality, and *Melaza* (2012) on the necessity of engaging in petty corruption in order to survive. In 2011, Cuba released its first "zombie" movie, *Juan de los Muertos*, a comedy in which the government attempts to cover up the existence of the living dead by alleging they were dissidents trying to overthrow the revolution.

The widespread popularity of hip-hop music forced official acceptance of the genre by the early part of the 2000s. As Cuban hip-hop evolved independently of US influence, its lyrics and themes became a distinctive contrast to the American genre. Instead of promoting sexual exploitation and consumption, Cuban artists focused on the problems of daily life. The music provided a way for the generation of the 1980s and 1990s "to speak out about racism, prostitution, police harassment, growing class differences, the difficulty of daily survival, and other social problems of contemporary Cuba."[68]

Another musical outlet came from folk singers. Cubans in the new millennium favored critical artists such as Carlos Varela. Many of his songs went right to the edge of what censors would allow and became wildly popular. Consider "William Tell," which recounts the famous story from the perspective of the archer's son. Tired of holding the apple on his head, the boy runs away. William Tell cannot understand why his son would abandon him, so the singer explains: "William Tell, your son has grown up / And now he wants to shoot the arrow himself."[69]

Given their experience with increased openness, artists were especially troubled in late 2018 when the government issued Decree 349, which would have allowed inspectors to close down any public performance or display if the artists were not members of a registered Cuban organization. Critics viewed the decree as a vehicle for censorship and succeeded in limiting its force. As a result, the Associated Press reported, "inspectors on their own will only be able to shut down shows in extreme cases, such as public obscenity, racist or sexist comment." The government also promised to consult with artists on the implementation of the decree.[70]

Inequality, Racism, and LGBTQ Rights

The Cuban government does not gather data on income distribution. Yet, increasing inequality is evident in the clothing Cubans wear, their choices in transportation and communication, the quality of their housing, and their different abilities to enjoy restaurants and recreation available only to those with a surplus of hard currency. Anthropologist Hope Bastian reports that inequality has not only created gaps in consumption. It has altered social relations, as local community ties have begun to disintegrate, generating new patterns of social stratification, and it has changed Cubans' values with a greater emphasis on materialism and individualism.[71]

Significantly, economic inequality emerged "along clearly visible racial lines," as sociologist Katrin Hansing has observed.[72] A greater proportion of darker-skinned than lighter-skinned Cubans were living in substandard housing, which made them unsuitable for rent to tourists, depriving them of one source of hard currency. Darker-skinned Cubans also lacked access to capital from remittances and suffered discrimination due to racist norms in hiring for the tourism industry. As a result, anti-racism organizations reemerged across the island after 2006, focusing on fields from legal rights to youth, culture, communications, and barrio-based community organizing.[73]

Journalist Jon Lee Anderson argues that considerable credit should be given to Alfredo Guevara, the founder of ICAIC, for helping to "usher in an era of gradual sexual glasnost" in producing *Fresa y Chocolate* (*Strawberries and Chocolate*) in 1993.[74] Directed by Tomás Gutiérrez Alea and Juan Carlos Tabío, the film examines the developing friendship between a gay artist and a committed young communist whose aim initially is to spy on the so-called deviant. *Fresa y Chocolate* not only portrays a gay Cuban sympathetically; it clearly criticizes the ways the government penalized homosexuality in the 1960s and the lame excuses the PCC offered to justify discrimination and repression of homosexuals.

The film's appearance marked a turning point for lesbian, gay, bisexual, transgender, and questioning (LGBTQ) Cubans. Less fearful about acknowledging their orientations, they began to gather openly in clubs, perform as transvestites, and speak out. While subsequent films reinforced their courage, unquestionably the most significant support came from Mariela Castro Espín, the director of the National Center of Sex Education (CENESEX) and daughter of Raúl and the late Vilma Espín. Established in 1989 with the aim of promoting sexual education, CENESEX was refocused by Mariela Castro in 2004 to concentrate on LGBTQ issues. Her crusade for LGBTQ rights engendered a national conversation, educated Cubans, and empowered the LGBTQ community. In 2008, she took to the streets to lead a parade on the International Day against Homophobia, and she prominently led the Gay Pride parade in subsequent years, though it was canceled in 2019.[75]

Since 2008, doctors have provided state-funded hormone replacement and sexual reassignment surgery (which Mariela Castro proposed in 2005). As an indication of changing attitudes, Fidel Castro acknowledged in 2010 the injustice of sending thousands of gay men and others deemed unfit for military service to labor camps known as Military Units to Aid Production in the mid-1960s. A 2013 law banned workplace discrimination based on sexual orientation.[76] However, as a result of an unprecedented public campaign undertaken by some evangelical churches and joined by the Catholic Church, the 2019 constitution does not include a provision that was in the July 2018 draft, which defined marriage as "the voluntary union of two legally qualified persons in order to live together in common" without any specification of gender.[77]

A CHANGED CUBA

The articles in *Cuba at the Crossroads* elaborate the general theme this chapter has presented. During the first two years of Raúl Castro's interim presidency and his two five-year terms as president, as well as in the first year of Miguel Díaz-Canel's presidency, Cuba experienced considerable change. There was a growth of small businesses; the *Lineamientos* began to open up the economy; greater freedom of expression contributed to an explosion of new films, music, art, and literature; international engagement created several new opportunities for development; eased travel restrictions enabled Cubans to work abroad and retain their property and rights on the island; and a new constitution provided a framework for greater political participation and a major updating of the economy. Yet by the end of 2019 many reforms remained in their planning stages, significant economic changes had not been instituted, the economy was stagnating, and international circumstances had brought new pressures.

When the National Assembly reelected Raúl as president in February 2013, he likely anticipated that his second term would involve knitting together the several components of a changed landscape so that he could turn over to his successor a fully revitalized Cuban Revolution. He had set in motion a program of economic "updating"; improved relations with the United States were on the horizon along with strong support from China and Western Hemisphere countries—despite the death of Hugo Chávez—and better relations with Europe; and a newly elected National Assembly had increased the representation of women. The remaining chapters in this book examine in detail the limited extent to which he was able to realize this vision, which has left Cuba at a crossroads of what to do next.

Chapter One

Politics

The Challenges Facing Cuba's New Leaders

William M. LeoGrande

Fidel Castro's death on November 25, 2016, prompted an outpouring of emotion among Cuban citizens, thousands of whom lined up well before dawn and stood for hours just to be able to pause for a few seconds to pay their respects in front of a 1950s photograph of Castro as a guerrilla in the Sierra Maestra mountains. Thousands more lined the streets to salute Castro's ashes as a caravan carried his remains the length of the island from Havana to Santiago, retracing the triumphal march he made in January 1959 after the fall of Fulgencio Batista's regime. Despite how discontented many Cubans were over their government's anemic economic performance, the state still seemed to retain significant legitimacy, especially among those old enough to remember pre-revolutionary Cuba. As Raúl Castro remarked, the founding generation enjoyed some "power of moral authority" based on their historic role.[1]

But the founding generation, "*los históricos*," were on their way out. Raúl Castro stepped down as president at the end of his second term in April 2018 and was slated to retire from his post as first secretary of the Communist Party in 2021. Because of recently adopted term limits, other members of the generation that won the revolution in 1959 were also retiring. The new generation stepping into their shoes faced a number of political challenges: a leadership divided about the pace and depth of social and economic change; a public impatient for economic improvement and skeptical of the government's ability to deliver it; and a deteriorating relationship with the United States.

For any state born in revolution, the first transfer of power to a new generation is momentous and fraught with the question of how the new rulers establish their legitimacy. More so in Cuba, where for decades Fidel Castro's charisma was a pillar of regime support. Raúl Castro tried to strengthen governing institutions to smooth the transition, and he elevated new leaders to responsible positions while the older generation was still in place to ensure stability and continuity. Nevertheless, without the legitimacy that comes from having founded the regime, Cuba's new leaders needed to establish their right to rule by superior performance—first and foremost by completing the restructuring of the economy and delivering on the promise of economic growth and a living wage. At the same time, they had to reassure people, as Raúl Castro repeatedly promised, that no one would be left behind and that the state would cushion or limit the growth of inequality.

THE SEVENTH PARTY CONGRESS

The Seventh Congress of the Communist Party of Cuba convened in April 2016 under a huge banner featuring a photograph of a younger, smiling Fidel Castro and the slogan "The Communist Party of Cuba is, now and forever, the party of the Cuban nation." A fragile Fidel briefly appeared in person wearing an Adidas jogging suit rather than his emblematic olive-green uniform. Alluding to his own mortality, he told the delegates that this would probably be his final appearance at such a gathering.[2] The following day, when the membership of the new Central Committee was announced, Fidel was not among them.

Generational change was high on the agenda, as it had been at the previous Party Congress in 2011, when Raúl Castro emphasized the need to build a contingent of experienced young men and women for the inevitable succession. To ease out the old guard, he introduced term limits for top government and party positions—no more than two five-year terms—and pledged to abide by the limit himself by stepping down as president in 2018. Castro reiterated the importance of rejuvenating the party. An aged leadership was "never positive," he said, reminding listeners that three leaders of the Soviet Communist Party died within months of one another a few years before its collapse. Henceforth, Castro proposed, sixty would be the maximum age for admission to the Central Committee, and seventy would be the maximum age for assuming any leadership position. Renovating the leadership would involve a "five-year period of transition to avoid doing things in haste," Castro said.[3]

The composition of the 2016 Central Committee included a large new cohort of younger members, while retaining a core of experienced elders, and had a more technocratic tilt, positioning it for the complex economic tasks ahead. Twenty-five percent of the old committee was dropped, but the membership was expanded from 116 to 142 to accommodate the addition of fifty-five younger members, all below the age of sixty, bringing the average age of the body down to 54.5. The new committee was 44.4 percent women, up from 41.7 percent in 2011 and just 13.3 percent in 1997; and 35.9 percent Afro-Cuban, up from 31.3 percent in 2011 and just 10.0 percent in 1997. The increased representation of women and Afro-Cubans better reflected their role in society and politics, connecting the party to these key constituencies.[4]

Members of the Central Committee typically hold other important posts in various state institutions. The relative bureaucratic influence of those institutions can be seen in the Central Committee's changing composition. The biggest increase in institutional representation in the new committee was for government officials working in economic and scientific fields, who represented 23.2 percent of the new Central Committee, up from just 19.8 percent in 2011. Presumably, these people are more technocratically minded and more likely to support economic reform. Representation of the party apparatus increased only slightly, to 32.4 percent of the committee, up from 31.0 percent in 2011. The armed forces were the big losers, comprising just 9.2 percent of the new membership, down from 13.8 percent in 2011.[5]

"PROSPEROUS AND SUSTAINABLE SOCIALISM"

The economy was a central focus of the 2016 Party Congress, just as it was in 2011 when Castro launched the "updating" of Cuba's antiquated Soviet-era economic model, seeking to replace it with a Cuban version of market socialism. The review of performance since the 2011 Congress was disheartening. Only 21 percent of the 313 economic proposals adopted in the "Guidelines of the Economic and Social Policy of the Party and the Revolution" had been fully implemented.[6] The annual GDP growth rate from 2001 to 2015 was just 2.8 percent, and wages were "unable to satisfy the basic needs of Cuban families," Castro0 acknowledged. The process of rationalizing state enterprises, which still produced about three-quarters of GDP, was hampered by managers who still had "the habit of waiting for instructions from above" instead of "encouraging initiative and entrepreneurship."[7]

The 2016 Congress approved a new document, the "Conceptualization of the Cuban Social and Economic Model of Socialist Development," a theoretical blueprint of what "prosperous and sustainable" socialism would look like once the economic transformation was complete.[8] It began with a frank assessment of Cuba's economic shortcomings: inadequate supplies of goods and services due to low productivity and poor planning, decaying infrastructure and obsolete technology due to inadequate investment, social inequality arising from the dual currency system, and the fact that state sector wages were not meeting basic needs. Such problems required profound economic change centered on raising productivity (¶ 29).

While the document laid out both the problems and the essential solutions clearly, it nevertheless reflected the tensions within the political elite about how the goal of increased productivity could be achieved, particularly the tension between the desire to retain the socialist character of the system and the recognition that markets and private property needed to play a greater role. For those who might worry that the reforms were the leading edge of capitalist restoration, the document repeatedly asserted the primacy of "socialist property of all the people in the fundamental means of production" as the dominant form of ownership (¶ 63), and the primacy of socialist planning as "the principal avenue for directing the economy" (¶ 67). But that reassurance was invariably paired with the assertion that the new model required "recognizing the heterogeneity of forms of property and management" (¶ 47) and "the objective existence of the market" (¶ 212).

The vision of Cuba's economic future laid out in the document was one in which the commanding heights of the economy (the "fundamental" means of production, "strategic sectors," and "axes" of development) remained under state control, but the state would gradually divest itself of other enterprises. Private property would exist, including foreign direct investment, and private businesses might even manage state property, but private enterprise would be strictly regulated. Markets would set most prices, but within limits established by state policy (¶ 240–43). Foreign investment would help stimulate development, but not at the expense of national sovereignty (¶ 86), and the state would not allow the emergence of a new class based on the "concentration of property and wealth" (¶ 176).

For the general citizenry, worried about what the economic reforms would mean for their standard of living, the document offered another set of reassurances. It reiterated the regime's commitment to providing universal health care, education, social security, citizen security, decent housing, and "state subsidies for families whose economic situation requires it" (¶ 69, 70, 277). Echoing what Raúl Castro had said on numerous occasions, the document promised there would be no "shock therapy" (¶ 315) and "no one will be left helpless" (¶ 71). Nevertheless, it also acknowledged that the reforms would produce a degree of inequality: there would be "differences in the income among those who work, depending on the quantity, quality, and complexity of their work and results" (¶ 302).

Reaching agreement within Cuba's leadership on the Conceptualization was apparently no easy task. Discussion began five years before the Seventh Party Congress, and the document went through eight drafts as a result of discussions within the Council of Ministers and the Communist Party's Political Bureau and Central Committee. Unlike the Guidelines adopted at the Sixth Party Congress, the Conceptualization document was not discussed at the base level of the party prior to the Party Congress. That was because, according to the daily newspaper, *Granma*, completing it "required more time than initially supposed,"[9] suggesting that the leadership was debating the finer points of it right up until the congress convened.

The lack of public discussion produced complaints by party members about the undemocratic character of having Congress delegates approve a blueprint for Cuba's future that the public had not even seen.[10] "The base of the party is angry, and rightly so," wrote scholar Esteban Morales. "We've gone backward in terms of democracy in the party, because we've forgotten about the base."[11] The uproar was serious enough that Castro announced the Conceptualization would only be approved provisionally until the public had an opportunity to debate it and suggest revisions. It was essential, he said at the close of the Party Congress, to "forge a consensus."[12]

Despite the calls for unity, Castro's plans to modernize Cuba's economy faced political opposition from the outset. Within the political elite, resistance came from people who, like Fidel, feared that concessions to the market were a slippery slope leading to capitalist restoration or even regime collapse, as happened in Eastern Europe and the Soviet Union. In a long, reflective speech at the University of Havana in November 2005, just a few months before he fell ill, Fidel warned that the idea "that socialism could be constructed with capitalist methods" was "one of the great historical errors."[13]

Yet that was precisely what Raúl was trying to do. The economic renovation program focused on expanding private enterprise, allowing greater sway for market forces, boosting productivity with wage incentives, and attracting foreign investment—capitalist methods all. Raúl attributed the slow pace of reform to bureaucratic resistance from those charged with implementing them. "The main obstacle we have faced . . . is the issue of outdated mentalities," Castro told the Party Congress.[14]

Eight months later, Castro reported that "frequent, excessive delays" in the bureaucratic approval of proposed foreign investment projects were crippling the search for foreign capital.[15] In the two and a half years since the new foreign investment law was adopted, only $1.3 billion in foreign direct investment had been approved—far short of the $2.5 billion per year goal.[16] "It is necessary to overcome, once and for all, the obsolete mentality of prejudices toward foreign investment," Castro insisted. "We must rid ourselves of unfounded fears of foreign capital; we are not heading toward, nor will we head toward capitalism, this is totally ruled out." Private property and markets were not incompatible with socialism, as the experiences of Vietnam and China proved.[17] The next day, *Granma*'s headline read, "Raúl: 'We Are Not Going Back, nor Will We Go Back, to Capitalism.'"[18]

For some cadres, ideological concerns were reinforced by self-interest. If state sector economic management was decentralized, and nonstrategic economic activity devolved to the private sector, the role of the central government bureaucracy would be much diminished. As central administrative structures contracted, so would the number of bureaucrats and the perquisites available to those who remained. Even for bureaucrats whose jobs were not at risk, it was galling to see the growing prosperity of private entrepreneurs benefiting from the reforms while government salaries remained inadequate. In the armed forces, where discontent would present a unique danger, the government tried to minimize it by expanding benefits, especially housing.[19] But civilian bureaucrats received no such relief from the effects of increasing inequality.

REGULATING THE PRIVATE SECTOR

By mid-2017, the government had concluded that the private sector's growth was out of control and represented a political problem. Speaking to the National Assembly in July 2017, Castro accused private businesses of "illegalities," including tax evasion and black-marketeering. He insisted that private enterprise would remain a permanent part of the economic landscape, but he warned of new regulations to come.[20] On August 1, the government announced that it was temporarily suspending the issuance of new licenses for some private occupations, including the most popular—private restaurants (*paladares*) and bed-and-breakfast rentals (*casas particulares*). A number of successful, high-profile businesses were closed for allegedly expanding into areas not authorized by their licenses.[21]

The accusations against the private sector were not untrue. Self-employment licenses were written so narrowly that businesses frequently operated beyond the scope of their letter. With no access to wholesale markets for supplies or equipment, entrepreneurs were often forced to trade on the black market. Tax rates were so high and the tax system so rudimentary that businesses felt compelled—and able—to evade taxes in order to stay open. The government set the rates unreasonably high knowing full well that people would only declare a portion of their income, thus creating a vicious circle of extortionate rates and rampant evasion. As Cuban economist Ricardo Torres pointed out, the problems with the private sector might be real, but part of the blame lay with government policies that failed to provide an environment in which businesses could operate successfully within the law.[22]

In July 2018, eleven months after the license suspensions, the government finally issued over one hundred pages of new regulations intended to minimize illegal behavior, protect public safety, enable the state to capture a greater share of the revenue generated by private businesses, and limit the growth of individual businesses in order to prevent the accumulation of wealth and property. For example, taxi drivers were required to buy gasoline from state service stations and retain receipts to prove they were not getting fuel illegally.[23] In the past, as much as half the fuel supply was siphoned off into the black market. To get a new license, prospective entrepreneurs had to prove that they obtained the investment capital for their start-up legally. Businesses had to keep their accounts in state banks to prevent tax evasion.

Some new rules provided consumer and worker protection, such as those governing food preparations in private restaurants and the requisite facilities for private day care. Businesses had to have a labor contract with employees to safeguard their rights, and discrimination on the basis of race, gender, or sexual orientation was explicitly prohibited. Other regulations limited the ability of private businesses to compete with the state sector. Tourist taxis had to work through state tourism agencies rather than operate independently. Private businesses were no longer allowed to work for foreign clients—a hard blow for Cuban computer programmers who had developed a market abroad.[24]

The most onerous new rules were those designed to limit the growth of individual businesses. Minimum taxes went up and tax rates increased as a business hired more employees, which was a disincentive to growth. Real estate agencies, language schools, and tutoring operations were no longer allowed to hire any employees. The 201 categories of permitted enterprises were consolidated into 123 categories that were more broadly defined, which was positive, but the initial regulations allowed an individual to hold only one license. Although only 9,657 of the 591,496 private businesses held multiple licenses, they were among the most successful.[25] Private restaurants, for example, had been limited to fifty seats, but some of Cuba's most famous spots got around that limit by obtaining additional licenses.

When the final regulations were announced in December 2018, however, the limit of one license per person and the fifty-seat limit for restaurants were dropped, along with some other revisions. "These adjustments reflect the government's intention to recognize the positive role played by self-employment workers in the updating of our economic model," explained Minister of Labor and Social Security Margarita González Fernández. The government was responding to the concerns voiced by the private sector and made changes based on "the opinion and experiences of those directly involved."[26]

The government also backtracked on a new law, Decree 349, requiring artists, musicians, and performers to register with the state and pay a 24 percent commission on their earnings from private engagements. It also prohibited work with pornographic or racist content, or work that promotes violence. The decree sparked widespread protests by artists who feared a return to the dark days of heavy state censorship in the 1970s. After dozens of meetings between various groups of artists and musicians and officials in the Ministry of Culture, the government agreed to modify the regulations to address their concerns.[27]

The tougher regulatory environment was unlikely to halt the growth of Cuba's private sector. Entrepreneurs had faced harsher conditions in the past and managed to *resolver*—to find ways to make things work. Moreover, the state needed a growing private sector to absorb the surplus labor being laid off from inefficient state enterprises, whether the party's ideological conservatives liked it or not. But friction between the state and private sector was clearly going to be an ongoing feature of the new Cuban model.

POLITICS AT THE GRASSROOTS

Cuba's leadership faced serious popular discontent over the dysfunctional state of the economy and, at the same time, popular fear of an uncertain future as the reform process transformed economic relations between citizen and state. The rationing system no longer provided sufficient sustenance, and state sector wages were too low to make up the difference. To make ends meet, most state sector workers had to have something on the side—"*por la izquierda*"—like selling pilfered state supplies on the black market or working a second job in the informal economy. The pervasiveness of the black market, generally tolerated by the government because the economy could not function without it, normalized illegality.[28] Opportunities for self-employment were closed off for most professions, leading many young, educated Cubans to emigrate. Castro's ambitious economic reform program initially raised hopes that the government would finally tackle these problems, but it had yet to significantly raise the standard of living of most Cubans.

In 2015, the Miami-based firm Bendixen and Amandi conducted a poll on the island and found that 79 percent of Cubans were dissatisfied with the economy. When asked what the Cuban people needed most, respondents answered that they needed an improved economy (48 percent) and an improved quality of life (24 percent). When asked what main thing they would like the government to do to improve things over the next five years, 54 percent said to improve economic opportunities.[29] A 2016 poll by NORC (formerly known as the National Opinion Research Center) at the University of Chicago found similar results. Asked to rate the country's economic condition, only 13 percent of Cubans rated it good or excellent, whereas 46 percent rated it poor or very poor. An overwhelming majority (95 percent) said that economic growth was a very important or extremely important goal for the coming decade.[30]

With such widespread and persistent discontent over the economy, it was no surprise that many people had a low opinion of the government's performance and were pessimistic about its ability to solve the country's problems. The Bendixen poll asked people how satisfied they were with the political system. Fifty-three percent replied dissatisfied, while 39 percent said they were satisfied. Asked if Cuba should have more than one political party, 52 percent said yes, 28 percent said one party was enough, and 20 percent did not respond. Support for multiple parties was higher among younger respondents: of those under age fifty, 59 percent said yes, and 23 percent said no. But those over age sixty narrowly favored the single-party system, 38 percent to 37 percent.

Asked their opinion of Raúl Castro, respondents were evenly divided: 47 percent positive, 48 percent negative. But here, too, the generation gap was wide. Cubans under fifty were more critical, with 52 percent holding a negative opinion of Castro, and 44 percent a positive one, whereas Cubans over sixty rated Castro favorably by a wide margin, 53 percent positive to 39 percent negative. Clearly, the near-euphoric enthusiasm of the revolution's early years left a lasting mark on those who lived through it, providing the regime with a base of support and legitimacy among that generation.[31] But just as clearly, the regime faced a legitimacy deficit, if not a legitimacy crisis, among younger generations who played no role in the regime's founding and who withheld their support because of the state's contemporary economic performance.

The contradiction between economic dynamics and political ones could be seen in microcosm in the problem of rising food prices. With private farmers able to sell to hotels, and hotels bursting with a tsunami of tourists, the supply of food in the free farmers' markets shrank in early 2016, and prices jumped.[32] Economic logic would dictate that higher prices would stimulate greater production in the long term, regardless of short-term consumer complaints. But that was not a political risk the government was willing to take. Instead, it forced farmers to sell more of their produce through the state distribution systems at controlled prices—a solution that pleased consumers but undercut incentives for farmers to raise production.

In the years after 1959, the Cuban regime's capacity to mobilize support lay in the principal mass organizations—the trade unions, women's federation, student federation, and the Committees for the Defense of the Revolution, which together included the vast majority of adult citizens. The economic crisis of the Special Period inflicted serious damage on these political arrangements.[33] Not only did it cause an erosion of popular faith in the government and in socialism as an ideology (a spiritual crisis that produced a resurgence of the Catholic Church), but it also weakened the institutional infrastructure of the state. The mass organizations, dependent on grassroots volunteers, began to wither away as people were forced to focus on economic survival. Organizations that had once served not only as the leadership's eyes and ears locally, but also as its arms and legs, carrying out government policy and fixing problems on the spot, no longer had the capacity to serve as "street-level bureaucrats."[34]

The 2014 documentary film *Canción de Barrio* followed musician Silvio Rodríguez's concert tour to some of Havana's poorest neighborhoods, where residents were interviewed about their lives. While the residents displayed admirable ingenuity in dealing with their harsh conditions, "*las organiza-ciones*" (state, party, and mass organizations) were noticeably absent and unresponsive. People in the barrios felt like they were on their own—"excluded people," as one woman described herself and her neighbors.[35]

These shortcomings hurt the party's image. In the Bendixen poll, 58 percent of respondents rated the party negatively, and only 32 percent positively. Younger Cubans were the most critical, with 65 percent rating the party negatively, and only 28 percent positively, although their elders were evenly divided, 43 percent positive and 43 percent negative.[36] Another indicator of the party's tenuous standing was an 18 percent decline in membership from 2011 to 2016—the first decline since the party was founded in 1965.[37]

The state's relationship with the public was changing in other ways as well. The leadership's admission that the old model of socialism Cuba had pursued for half a century was fatally flawed inevitably touched off debate among Cuba's highly educated population about what the future ought to look like. Raúl Castro himself gave this debate his blessing. As early as 2006, he told university students, "Sometimes people fear the word 'disagree,' but I say the more debate and the more disagreement you have, the better the decisions will be."[38] In 2012, speaking to the party cadre at the Party Conference, he returned to the theme of open debate, denouncing "false unanimity." "We need to accustom ourselves to expressing truths face to face, looking each other straight in the eye, to disagree and argue, to even disagree with what leaders say, when we believe that we are in the right."[39]

Cuban intellectuals accepted this invitation, launching spirited discussions, at first in print journals and magazines like *Espacio Laical*, *Vitral*, and *Palabra Nueva*, produced by the Catholic Church, and *Revista Temas*, a journal of social and cultural criticism that technically belonged to the Ministry of Culture but nevertheless tackled sensitive topics like inequality, racial discrimination, the role of religion, and the nature of socialist democracy. Even the official newspaper, *Juventud Rebelde*, began conducting investigative reports of official corruption and malfeasance.

As internet access and cell phone availability expanded, more and more Cubans had access to new sources of digital information and connected with one another via social media, spurring the growth of social networks that constituted an independent civil society beyond state control. By 2019, 5.4 million Cubans had cell phones and 2.5 million had 3G internet access.[40] Cuban authorities turned a blind eye to the creation of a wide variety of informal, independent, and technically illegal voluntary associations that sprang up. Blogs appeared—dissident, *oficialista*, and everything in between—carrying out debates and polemics in the evolving digital town square.[41] Independent journalists colonized the digital public sphere, launching digital magazines and news services. And for Cubans who still lacked internet access, "*el paquete*" (literally, "the package") offered a weekly smorgasbord of digital content at affordable prices on portable hard drives and thumb drives, distributed nationwide by hand by young entrepreneurs. [42]

Some senior Cuban officials voiced concerns that expanded internet access posed political risks, especially since the United States had repeatedly tried to use it as a channel for waging information warfare. In 2018, the Trump administration formed a Cuba Internet Task Force to explore ways to "expand freedom of expression" as part of the president's policy to undermine the Cuban government. [43]

In early 2017, ideological hard-liners in Havana launched a vitriolic online campaign against "centrism," which they derided as the belief that one could combine the positive attributes of socialism and the positive attributes of capitalism to create a third way. The anti-centrist polemics targeted moderate critics of the regime—especially those with an online presence, including the "laboratory of ideas" *Cuba Posible*, run by the former editors of the Catholic Church magazine *Espacio Laical*. [44] At first, the attacks on "social democrats" and "neo-counterrevolutionaries" were confined to unofficial blogs, but in June and July, the Communist Party's newspaper, *Granma,* ran several opinion columns endorsing the anti-centrism campaign. [45] Cuban intellectuals fought back, however, and the public campaign subsided after Silvio Rodríguez denounced the attacks as "an infantile disorder," citing Lenin's polemic against left-wing communism. [46] Nevertheless, targets of the attacks continued to suffer harassment, and *Cuba Posible* finally closed down in May 2019.

A CAREFULLY CALIBRATED SUCCESSION

For a man stepping down after half a century at the apex of Cuba's government—first as vice president and armed forces minister, then as president—Raúl Castro was in good humor, looking relaxed and happy in April 2018 when he handed the presidency to his designated successor, fifty-eight-year-old Miguel Díaz-Canel. Departing from the prepared text of his valedictory speech to Cuba's National Assembly, Castro cracked jokes, reminisced about the revolution, and quipped that he planned to travel more, "since I'm supposed to have less work to do." [47]

Castro also gave the clearest explanation yet of the succession process he envisioned. Castro and octogenarian José Machado Ventura would remain the first and second secretaries of the Communist Party until the next Party Congress in 2021, in order to ensure "a secure transition and apprenticeship" for the new president. After that, Díaz-Canel, if he had done a good job, would become head of the party as well as the government. When his second term as president concluded, Díaz-Canel, like Raúl before him, would serve another three years as party leader to ensure that the next presidential transition went smoothly.

The central theme of the National Assembly meeting was continuity. Díaz-Canel began his inaugural speech with a paean to Raúl Castro's leadership and a promise to continue his policies, especially "updating" the economy, which Díaz-Canel lauded as "profound and essential structural and conceptual changes" to Cuba's socialist model. He declared that Cuban foreign policy would "remain unchanged," and he cited the restoration of diplomatic relations with the United States as one of Castro's achievements—a signal that Cuban leaders still hoped to improve relations with Washington, despite the deterioration of ties after President Donald Trump took office. [48]

To allay his fellow citizens' concerns about the presidential succession, Díaz-Canel pledged that Raúl Castro, in his role as first secretary of the Communist Party, would continue to "lead the most important decisions for the present and the future of the nation," a promise that drew prolonged applause. That declaration was reminiscent of Raúl's inaugural speech in 2008, when he promised to consult Fidel on all major issues—a new president hoping to share his predecessor's mantle of legitimacy.

Díaz-Canel stressed the theme of unity, within the party and within the broader public, while promising a more collective and participatory leadership style—a necessary virtue for a president who lacked the inherent authority of being a Castro. Harkening back to Cuba's struggle for independence, Díaz-Canel called unity the nation's "most valuable and sacred force" for the defense of its sovereignty. He repeatedly asserted the need for greater popular participation in government and a government more responsive to the popular will. Serving the people's interests was the government's "raison d'être," he declared. He spent the first few months of his presidency traveling around the country on a get-acquainted tour, meeting with local and provincial officials. In December 2018, he ordered his ministers to appear on the *Mesa Redonda* television interview program to explain their work. For most Cubans, it was the first time they had seen high government officials being questioned, albeit politely, about contemporary problems. [49] Soon after, Díaz-Canel and almost all the ministers opened Twitter accounts through which Cuban citizens could sound off directly to their leaders.

Born in 1960, Díaz-Canel represented the ascension of the generation born after the triumph of the revolution. His rise exemplified Raúl Castro's commitment to institution-building, promoting people on the basis of experience and merit, as opposed to his brother Fidel's penchant for elevating promising but inexperienced young people to top positions for which they were often unprepared—people Raúl derisively called "test-tube leaders." Díaz-Canel, by contrast, was a seasoned, pragmatic politician who rose through the ranks of the Communist Party, serving for a decade as party first

secretary—the highest political position—in his home province of Villa Clara and as first secretary in Holguín for six years. He joined the Communist
Party's Central Committee in 1991, and the Political Bureau in 2003. At
forty-three, he was the youngest person ever named to the party's highest
body. In 2009, Díaz-Canel was brought to Havana to head the Ministry of
Higher Education. In 2012, he was named one of several vice presidents, and
in 2013 as first vice president and likely successor to the presidency.

In the provinces, he earned a reputation as an honest, efficient manager
and an enemy of corruption. Shortly after assuming the presidency, he
launched an anti-corruption campaign, calling corruption "the principal enemy of the revolution."[50] Although his speeches tended to be flat and unin-
spiring, in small groups he was said to be relaxed, humorous, and willing to
listen. When Cuba was plagued by fuel shortages during the economic crisis
of the 1990s, he abandoned his official car and security detail to ride to work
on a bicycle, endearing him to his constituents.

He also appeared to be socially tolerant. He was a Beatles fan in the
1970s, a time when their music was banned as an expression of bourgeois
decadence. In Villa Clara, he defended Cuba's first LGBTQ club and cultural
center, El Mejunje, against critics who wanted it shut down.[51] Shortly after
Díaz-Canel was named first vice president, a controversy erupted over the
censorship of an independent yet generally pro-government blog, *La Joven
Cuba,* at the University of Matanzas. Díaz-Canel weighed in on the side of
the bloggers and in favor of allowing open debate online for the simple
reason that in the long run, the state could not control it anyway. "Banning
something is almost an impossible illusion. It makes no sense," he explained.
"Today, the news from all sides, good and bad, manipulated and true, and
half-true, circulates on the networks, reaches people, people are aware of it."
He criticized Cuba's official press for its unwillingness to tackle real problems and he posed for a photograph with the bloggers.[52]

His history seemed to place Díaz-Canel squarely in the camp of party
moderates—until someone leaked a video of him speaking to a closed meeting of Communist Party members in Havana on February 13, 2017. In a
lengthy presentation, he recited the full litany of conservative positions. He
echoed the familiar charge that dissidents were all mercenaries paid by the
United States, but he extended his attack to independent voices that advocat-
ed reforming the socialist system rather than replacing it: Cuba Emprende, a
project of the Catholic Church and the Miami-based Cuba Study Group that
provided business education to would-be entrepreneurs; *OnCuba*, a Miami
media company with press credentials in Havana; and *Cuba Posible*, the self-
described laboratory of ideas that published a wide variety of social, economic, and political analysis and came under attack by conservatives in their
campaign against centrism. Contrary to his earlier defense of online debate,
Díaz-Canel promised the audience of party faithful that *OnCuba* would be

silenced. "We will shut it down it," he said. "And let the scandal ensue. Let them say we censor, it's fine. Everyone censors."[53] (*OnCuba* was not shut down, however.)

Did the pirated video reveal Díaz-Canel to be a wolf in sheep's clothing, a party hard-liner who had been masquerading as a moderate? Or was he a sheep who had to growl to reassure the wolves that he was up to the job of leading the pack? As president, Díaz-Canel had to maintain a delicate balancing act among the diverse voices and contending interests that comprise Cuba's political elite.

Once Díaz-Canel assumed the presidency, however, he maintained a laser-like focus on the economy. When President Donald Trump stepped up sanctions against Cuba in 2019, Díaz-Canel delegated the job of responding to Foreign Minister Bruno Rodríguez so as not to distract from his own message that Cubans needed to fix their economy themselves. He even began using the term "internal blockade" to refer to the bureaucratic impediments stifling economic growth—a phrase that originated with Miami exiles in response to the idea that the US embargo was responsible for Cuba's economic problems. Díaz-Canel, echoing Raúl Castro's previous complaints, criticized bureaucratic obstacles to foreign investment, the lack of officials' appreciation for the importance of the private sector, and low productivity in the state sector. It was essential, he told the National Assembly in July 2019, to "open up" the national economy and "untie the knots that bind it."[54]

A series of external shocks pushed the economy toward recession during Díaz-Canel's first year in office. The shortfall in oil shipments from Venezuela created a fuel shortage and necessitated cutbacks in electricity consumption in state agencies and enterprises. The withdrawal of doctors from Brazil after the election of far-right president Jair Bolsonaro reduced hard currency earnings by several hundred million dollars. President Trump's restrictions on travel caused a shortfall in tourism revenue, and declining prices reduced the receipts from nickel exports. The result was a severe shortage of hard currency that limited import capacity, producing a shortage of consumer goods. In May 2019, the government introduced a new rationing system at market prices for certain basic commodities, mostly foods. The shortages sparked public fears of a new Special Period—the decade-long depression that followed the collapse of the Soviet Union—despite the government's insistence that things would not get that bad.[55] The economy's weakness underscored the urgency of reform but at the same time made it politically more perilous.

Díaz-Canel's speech on July 26, 2019, the main revolutionary holiday commemorating the attack on Moncada barracks in 1953 that began the revolution, praised the retiring historic generation and sounded patriotic themes. The battle for the economy, he argued, was critical to the defense of national sovereignty in the face of escalating US economic attacks. Washington's aim was to impoverish ordinary Cubans, turning them against their government and against one another. Enduring the resulting hardships and fighting to improve production was a matter of patriotic duty in the face of foreign aggression.[56] Díaz-Canel's appeals were a tried and true strategy of mobilizing nationalism against the US threat in order to rally the country behind the leadership, a strategy dating to the earliest years of the revolutionary government.

THE NEW CONSTITUTION

On July 21, 2018, just three months after Miguel Díaz-Canel's inauguration, he unveiled the draft of a new constitution to the National Assembly.[57] Once the assembly approved the draft, it was circulated for grassroots debate, after which a revised version came back to the National Assembly for approval in December and was then submitted to the public in a referendum in February 2019.

The avowed reason for revamping the constitution was to bring it into accord with the economic reforms spelled out in the 2011 Guidelines and the 2016 Conceptualization documents, which together constitute the blueprint for a transition to market socialism. Cuba's 1976 constitution, adopted at the height of Cuba's adherence to a Soviet model of central planning, reflected "historical circumstances, and social and economic conditions, which have changed with the passing of time," Raúl Castro said.[58]

Nevertheless, two key tenets of the old charter remained unchanged: (1) the new constitution reaffirmed the commitment to a socialist system in which state property predominates and Cubans are guaranteed free, universal social services; and (2) the Communist Party retained its leading role as sole political representative of the Cuban nation.

The most important constitutional changes for the economy were the legalization of private enterprise and employment, a prohibition on expropriating private property except for public purposes with compensation, and a guarantee for foreign direct investment.[59] Although private business had been allowed since 1992 under "self-employment" licenses, the private sector had been on shaky legal ground. Cuba's old constitution did not explicitly recognize private economic property other than land owned by small farmers, and it prohibited private businesses from hiring wage labor. Over the years, the fortunes of Cuba's small businesses waxed and waned with shifting political winds, creating tremendous uncertainty and driving many enterprises out of business or underground.[60] Having a firm legal foundation was a major step forward for the private sector, despite the tough new regulations announced just before the assembly meeting.

The most significant constitutional change in the structure of the government was the creation of the new post of prime minister. Before the revolution, Cuba had a presidential system with a subordinate prime minister. When Fidel Castro became prime minister in 1959, his personal authority as leader of the revolution reduced the presidency to a ceremonial post. The 1976 constitution restored the presidency to preeminence and abolished the post of prime minister. Despite Castro's long working hours and meticulous attention to detail, even he had trouble keeping tabs on the work of some two dozen ministries, especially is his later years. His aide Carlos Lage, executive secretary of the Council of Ministers, emerged as something of a de facto prime minister in the 1990s.

Díaz-Canel immediately demonstrated that he would be much more publicly visible and engaged than his predecessor, making it even more essential that he have help managing the day-to-day affairs of government. Supervising the ministries was especially important since getting the reluctant bureaucracy to implement Raúl Castro's economic reforms had been a constant problem. Other structural changes in the government appeared designed to more clearly separate legislative and executive branch functions. Overlapping membership between the Council of Ministers and the National Assembly's Council of State was prohibited, and the position of president of the republic was separated from the presidency of the Council of State. (The Council of State serves as the executive committee of the National Assembly and has the power to issue decree laws between assembly meetings.)

Provincial legislative assemblies are to be replaced by provincial councils composed of the presidents of the municipal assemblies and municipal mayors. Executive authority is vested in a governor appointed by the president and approved by the National Assembly. At the local level, the president of the elected municipal assembly and the head of local administration can no longer be the same person, and local governments are slated to be given greater autonomy to deal with local problems as they see fit.

From August to November, some 8.9 million Cubans debated the draft in their workplaces, neighborhoods, and schools. Party members were ordered not to argue with even the most radical proposals for amendments, and the ensuing debates were vigorous. Some of the main topics: whether the president and state governors should be directly elected; whether the concentration of wealth and property should be allowed; whether terms limits and age limits for leaders were a good idea; and whether the Communist Party should be subordinated to the constitution and hence the law. But the article drawing the most attention and debate was one recognizing same-sex marriage.

Mariela Castro, Raúl's daughter, succeeded in her effort to have the draft constitution recognize same-sex marriage, but the proposal sparked an unprecedented public political opposition campaign led by some elements in the evangelical churches and joined by the Catholic Church.[61] Not only did church leaders speak out against the provision, believers put up posters reading, "I'm in favor of the family as God created it" and "Marriage is the voluntary union between a man and a woman."[62] LGBTQ rights advocates countered with posters of their own. In the town hall meetings to discuss the draft constitution, the same-sex marriage issue was the most contentious—so much so that the government pulled the provision from the draft constitution and proposed to consider it later in the upcoming revision of the Family Code.[63] Then in May 2019, the government abruptly canceled the twelfth annual March against Homophobia on the grounds that it was inappropriate in light of "new tensions in the international and regional context." Organized via social media, more than one hundred LGBTQ activists marched anyway until they were stopped by police, who made several arrests.[64] Chastened by the churches' vehement opposition to same-sex marriage and their ability to mobilize opposition, the government retreated.

No comparable independently organized public mobilization campaign around a political issue had been allowed in Cuba since the early 1960s. The government's willingness to tolerate the churches' campaign against a policy that the party, the state, and the new president had all explicitly endorsed suggested a new openness to public debate. The government's willingness to respond by changing policy, coming at the same time as the government's regulatory concessions to the private sector and artists, suggested a new responsiveness to special interest groups, at least on issues that did not question the basic structure of the Cuban system. Yet once the precedent of a successful organized campaign was established, it could prove hard for the state to prevent future campaigns around more sensitive issues.

Dissidents mounted a social media campaign (#YoVotoNo) opposing the new constitution and urging people to vote against the draft in the February 2019 referendum. However, most of the tweets in support of the campaign came from people outside the island, who would not be voting in any case. Voters approved the constitution overwhelmingly, 86.9 percent voting yes, 9.0 percent voting no, and 4.2 percent spoiling or leaving their ballots blank. Turnout was 90.1 percent of registered voters, about the same as in the 2018 National Assembly elections, but relatively low compared to the turnout in prior elections, despite a major state media campaign to get out the vote.[65]

CONCLUSION: THE POLITICAL ECONOMY OF REFORM

Díaz-Canel's ascendance to the presidency of Cuba in April 2018 represented the final stage of Raúl Castro's carefully calibrated succession plan replacing the "historic" generation that founded the revolutionary regime with a new generation of leaders committed to carrying forward the core policies Raúl put in place during his ten years in office. The new constitution established the legal framework for a market socialist system in which the private sector and foreign investment would play a major role but would still be subordinate to the state sector and socialist planning. How well this hybrid system would work in practice remained to be seen.

Díaz-Canel's promise of a more open and responsive government catalyzed a robust constitutional debate and a surge in public expression by outspoken constituencies unhappy with various government policies, from artists and *cuentapropistas* to evangelical pastors. The government's willingness to adjust policy in the face of such criticism opened new space for Cuban civil society, and the expansion of internet access provided new tools and venues for organizing politics outside the regime.

The economy continued to be the top priority for Cuba's new leaders, just as it had been ever since Raúl Castro launched his reforms in 2011. Despite the gradual growth of private business and foreign investment, the bulk of GDP was still produced by a state sector that still suffered many of the problems that had plagued it for decades. If the goal of Cuban leaders was to raise productivity and the standard of living, tackling inefficiencies in the state sector was a necessary task, despite its difficulty and the political sensitivities involved.

The political risk of not pushing ahead with the economic reform program was arguably higher. Economic hardship continued to be the main source of complaints at the grassroots, and the longer economic growth remained anemic, the more disenchanted people became with the government's performance. That latent discontent, together with a growing sense of grievance over increasingly visible inequality, posed a significant political challenge to Cuba's political elite. As a new generation of Cuban leaders sought to establish their legitimacy, the state of the economy stood as the key to their success or failure.

Chapter Two

Cuba's Economy

Reforms and Delays, 2014–2018

Ricardo Torres

The process of updating the Cuban economic model formally began when the Communist Party of Cuba (Partido Comunista de Cuba, PCC), in its Sixth Congress of April 2011, adopted a resolution approving the *Lineamientos*, a set of socioeconomic policy "guidelines" for the country's development.[1] In April 2016, the Seventh Party Congress approved three documents that would guide the reform over the next five years: the new *Lineamientos*, a "Conceptualization of the Cuban Social and Economic Model of Socialist Development," and the "National Development Plan to 2030."[2]

Even before the start of the Sixth Congress, a number of modifications with strong impact on day-to-day life had already been introduced. In 2008, Cuban nationals were authorized to purchase mobile phone lines and stay at hotels previously restricted to foreign tourists. In 2009, public access to the internet, albeit limited, was approved. In the economic realm, the government took several steps to activate idle arable land and increase food production to reduce imports. In 2010, the sale of building materials was deregulated.

Shortly after the Sixth Party Congress, additional reforms were enacted. In 2011, Cuban nationals were authorized to trade their homes and vehicles. In 2013, overseas travel was liberalized. The same year, the creation of cooperatives outside of agriculture was authorized.

Assessing the progress of Cuba's reforms, branded as *actualización* ("updating"), since 2014, this chapter reviews policy initiatives, discusses overall economic performance, analyzes governmental responses to economic difficulties, and highlights the main points and economic implications of the new Cuban constitution.

NO HASTE AND MUCH PAUSE

Cuba went from adopting major policy initiatives to nearly a full stop in economic reforms by early 2016, as recognized by the government in a Council of Ministers meeting in March 2018. Cuban authorities argued that this was to be expected given the fact that initial steps were the easiest and some changes had not proceeded as anticipated. The trajectory of reform was also affected by transformational external events like the thaw with the United States, economic setbacks in Venezuela, and in late 2018 the end of the Cuban doctors program in Brazil. At the same time, the political scene was affected by the Seventh Party Congress in April 2016; the passing of Fidel Castro, Cuba's top political figure for over fifty years; the rise of a new generation of leaders to the country's top positions in 2018; and the discussion of a new constitution in the last few months of the same year. In terms of the pace of change and the nature of policy initiatives, the period since 2014 can be divided into two main phases. From 2014 to 2015, most changes were in line with the idea of reforming fundamental elements of the economic model. Beginning in early 2016, reforms almost stopped and policies became more restrictive, with the possible exception of foreign investment.

By 2014, attention increasingly focused on foreign investment, for which the old framework was at odds with the change in language put forward by the *Lineamientos*. The new language labeled Foreign Direct Investment (FDI) as a key component of the nation's economic strategy. Cuba first enacted a foreign investment law as early as 1995; however, the role played by FDI had been small. Compared with other countries, Cuba attracted only modest amounts of foreign capital.[3] In a centrally planned economy with predominantly state ownership in which the development of market relationships is still limited, investment is effectively controlled by the government, which restricts foreign participation to particular sectors or forms of investment deemed by the government to serve that national interest. But despite these constraints, Cuba's current medium- and long-term economic and social development strategy now considers foreign investment to be an integral element of national investment, rather than merely a complement to it.

Two new laws were especially significant. At the end of 2013, Decree-Law No. 313 created a unique Special Development Zone (ZDEM) at Mariel harbor, west of Havana. It was followed in 2014 by a new foreign investment law (Law 118). Taken together, these laws offer increased tax incentives, infrastructure built for investors in the Mariel Zone, and greater flexibility in the state employment agency's operation than the previous FDI structure provided. The government now appears willing to compensate investors in some areas, such as taxation and infrastructure, for its unwillingness to compromise on more sensitive issues like hiring practices, approval delays, and lack of transparency.

The year 2014 ended with the unprecedented announcements on December 17 by the US and Cuban presidents that relations would be normalized. In January and September 2015, the United States introduced modifications to the policy of sanctions aimed at expanding the possibilities of trade, investment, financial links, and travel. In May 2015, Cuba was removed from the US State Department's list of states that sponsor terrorism (which lifted some financial restrictions). That summer, both countries reopened embassies, and agreements were signed to restore direct mail and commercial flights.

While direct economic relations remained limited, this dynamic positively affected the number of Americans visiting Cuba and, predictably, the flow of capital in the form of remittances. In addition, the indirect effect on third countries was remarkable; the US-Cuba rapprochement stimulated tourism, finance, and investments from elsewhere. One of the areas of benefit for Cuba was the restructuring of the external debt with the member countries of the Paris Club.

In the wake of the 2009–2010 financial crisis, the Cuban government decided to start restructuring the country's foreign debt and improving its credit worthiness.[4] Since then, Cuba has significantly reduced its foreign indebtedness through bilateral negotiations of its long-term debt with major creditors, such as Japan, Russia, Mexico, and China. In all these cases, at least 70 percent of the total debt claims was written off and the repayment of remaining debt was rescheduled on acceptable terms. In December 2015, an agreement was made with the Paris Club to finally settle Cuba's debt of $11.1 billion. Seventy-six percent of this debt was written off and an eighteen-year repayment schedule was established for the remaining claims. It can be argued that the agreement was possible because US-Cuban relations had improved significantly.

Improving ties with the United States, and the great attention the process received from the Cuban government, may have partially concealed the internal contradictions suffered as a result of Cuba's economic reforms. Complaints in the December 2015 session of the National Assembly about rising food prices led to a partial reversal of agricultural reforms, especially the ability of producers and intermediaries to set prices freely according to market conditions. In April, new regulations went into effect introducing price caps and granting a greater role to Acopio, the state agency with a monopoly on marketing agricultural products, an agency whose inefficiency had been regarded as an obstacle to progress not so long before. In addition, in an attempt to curb social criticism, some prices for goods sold in convertible pesos were cut just before the start of the 2016 Party Congress. This was contradictory given that the country had begun to confront serious problems in its balance of payments, which would necessarily result in restrictions on imports, the main source of the products sold in these stores. The price cuts could be justified if an increase in foreign exchange earnings had occurred, but in practice, the opposite was happening.

April 2016 was a turning point in the process of economic reform. The apparent logic observed until then, based on the need for changes to improve economic performance, was set aside. The market and the participation of the non-state sector were considered responsible for the spike in prices and their consequent regressive effect on the distribution of wealth. In spite of the economic benefits, improving relations with the United States also generated reservations in influential circles in the government.

The combination of the two resulted in stalled reforms. However, at least on the formal political level, the Party Congress left some positive elements for the future of the reform. It recognized that only 22 percent of the 2011 "Guidelines" had been completely fulfilled, and it approved two new documents to replace the first generation of Guidelines. First was the Conceptualization, a theoretical and political document that described the general outline of Cuba's future model. Second was the 2030 National Development Plan, which provided a concrete roadmap for the following fifteen years. This document presumes the release of a second part, not yet completed, that will set the quantitative goals to be achieved during the period.

One key feature that stands out is the recognition that the Cuban model's sustainability depends directly on achieving greater development, which in turn is tightly linked to economic growth. The model leaves ample room for forms of property other than those owned by the state, including the recognition of private ownership over means of production, a first since 1959. A clear distinction is also made between property and management. In addition, the model legitimizes a shift toward more indirect means of state intervention in the economy. One section goes so far as to declare that "the state will concentrate on the functions appropriate to it, such as planning, regulating, conducting, and controlling the process of economic and social development."[5]

The 2030 National Development Plan is an ambitious proposal of great reach. According to the plan, development is examined through the so-called strategic axes, understood as the critical areas of transformation. It is an incomplete proposal though, because indicators, gaps, and goals remain to be elaborated, as do the corresponding financing needs and possible sources.

However, by the time the final versions of those documents were released in 2017, it was apparent that priorities had shifted and the reform had been put on hold. A deteriorating environment domestically and internationally introduced doubts and hesitation into the government's plans.

In July 2016, the government recognized that the country was facing growing stress in its external finances and austerity measures were necessary, including but not limited to forced energy savings in the public sector and stricter control over imports. In November came the news about the US presidential elections, won by the Republican candidate. Most experts were expecting a different result, and in both capitals, supporters of US-Cuban engagement had hoped to have at least four more years to cement the new relationship.

Since the start of 2017, things have gone from bad to worse. In June of that year, President Donald Trump announced a policy change aimed at partially dismantling President Barack Obama's Cuba policy legacy. On August 1, a Cuban Ministry of Labor and Social Security resolution, published in the Official Gazette that same day, established that temporarily no new licenses for private-sector businesses would be issued for a variety of activities and that changes would be introduced in the *cuentapropistas* (self-employed) business environment. To justify that decision, a wide range of reasons were given, among them tax evasion, the use of illegally obtained raw materials, the imprecision and insufficiency of controls, and deficiencies in contracting for the supply of services or products by individual entrepreneurs, cooperatives, and private companies.

More than eleven months later, on July 10, 2018, Cuba's Official Gazette published numerous new rules that included five decrees-laws, one decree, and fourteen resolutions, covering a grand total of 129 pages of changes in the relevant regulatory framework for the country's self-employed. This new episode in the endless zigzag around the private sector was announced under the euphemistic title of "Policy for the Perfection of Self-Employment." The overwhelming majority of the changes introduced constituted new restrictions on the exercise of these activities.

The new course taken has had negative repercussions at the socioeconomic level. In an economy facing a precarious fiscal scenario, millions of pesos were lost in taxes not collected when the state stopped issuing new licenses. The *cuentapropistas* pay an array of taxes, which includes a sales tax and taxes for the labor force, personal income, and social security. Although data is not available showing the amount that *cuentapropistas* contribute, it can be assumed that they pay an overwhelming part of total personal income taxes the government collects, based on the explosive growth of private-sector taxpayers until 2017, numbers that had tripled after 2009. Meanwhile, budget revenues (personal income tax) grew more than 4.8 times. On this basis, it can be estimated there was a minimum deficit (given that other taxes have not been considered) on the order of 900 million pesos. To put it in perspective, this amount is almost equivalent to what was spent on community projects and personal services in 2016.

From the start, when some of the new policies were announced, there was widespread discontent, including in academic sectors. It awakened an activism that prompted the attention of the authorities. In an unusual decision, especially because of the sensitivity of the issue, Cuban officials reversed some of the regulations related to self-employment work just before they went into effect in December 2018.

Specifically, the rules that denied Cubans the possibility of engaging in more than one kind of approved work activity and limited coffee shops, restaurants, and bars to fifty chairs were scrapped. Since then, the chair limit has been determined by the capacity of the premises in question. Regarding another highly sensitive issue, business bank accounts are still required, but with greater flexibility as to how large they must be, depending on the business's size. The decision-making process that led to the adoption of these regulations was opaque from the very beginning: the policy of "perfecting" self-employment was not and has not been shared with the public.

It is worth noting, however, that complaints of tax evasion and the purchase of stolen or "shady" goods are common concerns anywhere in the world. Self-employment in Cuba is part of a larger system whose failures cannot be attributed only to this sector.

Unfortunately, the experiment with transportation in Havana proceeded as initially announced. New regulations on private taxis or *almendrones* were met with a kind of passive resistance. As a result, the number of private cars serving the city dropped, as many failed to meet the new technical standards or decided to wait until the business climate improved. The reduced supply quickly translated into higher prices and fewer alternatives for people to move around in a city whose public transportation system has long been inadequate.

DISAPPOINTMENT AS A NORM

The economic reform initiated under the government of Raúl Castro has been the dominant political process since at least 2008, but its economic results lag behind the ideological and political implications. The government has devoted energy and time to this process, creating new structures such as the Implementation and Development Commission charged with overseeing the execution of the reforms. Even a cursory review of the speeches and public interventions of the previous president and his cabinet leaves few doubts that "*actualización*" of the economy has been the dominant focus.

Unfortunately, when analyzing the economic performance and structural problems that mark the development of the nation, the transformation has been much more superficial. The most telling example of this is that much of 2019 was marked by an acute balance-of-payments crisis that harshly affected links with Cuba's main external partners, resulting in a recurring shortage of products of all kinds, including essential goods like eggs and bread flour. Table 2.1 summarizes the main economic indicators for the 2014–2018 period.

These figures show very low average economic growth, well below the needs of a country of Cuba's size and level of development. This performance is not compatible with a sustained improvement in the living conditions of a majority of Cubans. In the Cuban model, inflation and the unemployment rate as reported do not transmit the information they carry in other contexts, so they must be interpreted with great caution. The consumer price index does not include price changes in convertible pesos; so its recent evolution would not adequately reflect the price dynamics in markets of great importance for the daily life of large segments of the population. Food and transport are two sectors in which there has been a clear upward trend, which is not sufficiently weighted in this index.

In relation to the unemployment rate, the increase in the informal economy and the current demographic characteristics of an aging population suggest that the rate of economic activity (i.e., the proportion of the working population with a formal job) would be a more useful measure of certain trends in the labor market. This indicator has been showing a systematic decline since 2011, when it went from 76.1 percent to 63.8 percent in 2018. Another cause of this increase is the emerging phenomenon of Cubans who have emigrated but retain their residency status. Reflecting the challenges facing the nation since 2016, the total working-age population has begun to shrink in absolute terms. Currently, there are fewer formal employees who contribute directly to the central budget, from which social services are financed for the population as a whole.

Table 2.1 Selected Macroeconomic Indicators, Cuba (2014–2018)

	Annual Growth Rates (%)[a]				
	2014	2015	2016	2017	2018
GDP (constant prices, 1997)	1.0	4.3	0.5	1.8	2.2
Inflation[b]	2.1	2.8	−2.9	0.6	2.4
Unemployment rate	2.7	2.4	2.0	1.7	1.7
Investment (current prices)	−8.9	24.9	10.2	23.8	15.4
Gross capital formation (% of GDP)	7.6	9.4	9.6	10.3	12.0
Exports of goods and services (current prices)	−4.2	−16.1	−8.4	2.9	3.0
Imports of goods and services (current prices)	11.1	9.2	10.9	0.7	11.1
Trade balance (USD millions)	3,947	2,350	2,463	2,774	1,936
Budget balance (% of GDP)	−2.2	−5.8	−6.6	−8.6	−8.1

Source: Author's calculations based on data from the Office of National Statistics, *Anuario Estadístico de Cuba* (La Habana, Oficina Nacional de Estadística e Información, 2005–2016).
[a] except otherwise indicated
[b] inclusive only of prices in Cuban pesos (CUP)

In this period, the country managed to maintain a surplus trade balance, mainly due to falling imports matching the drop in exports. This is, in perspective, an unsustainable trajectory with a high cost to growth.

In 2015, the growth in Gross Domestic Product (GDP) stood at 4.4 percent. That year there was more-balanced performance at the industry level: all branches showed increases in their activity, although some did not grow at the expected pace. International tourism benefited particularly from the new relationship with the United States, which had a positive impact on other markets as well.

Already in 2016, the economy began to slow down and the outlook became even more adverse in the second half of the year. This period was marked by the impact of the austerity measures announced by the government in July and the weakness of general economic activity, with the exception of international tourism. Energy rationing (due to the shortfall in oil shipments from Venezuela), although discretionally managed to avoid blackouts and impacts on strategic activities, had recessive effects. The planned restrictions in imports and investments accelerated the downward spiral. International tourism was the only large industry that gave the economy a boost in 2016. However, Canada (the main source of tourists) decreased by 6.7 percent, a trend that continued into 2018. The cause of the decline is still unclear, but the Ministry of Tourism in Cuba points to the depreciation of the Canadian dollar against the US dollar. The Cuban convertible peso (CUC) is pegged to the US dollar, and prices are set in CUCs. As a result, when the American currency appreciates, travel to Cuba becomes more expensive. In addition, the government was very conservative in taking on new international loans in order to avoid debt levels beyond its actual ability to re-pay them.

Amid growing external financial constraints, international tourism continued to be one of the pillars of the country's economic performance in 2017, but it suffered setbacks in the last two quarters. That was the year of the takeoff in the number of cruise passengers, with estimated arrivals of almost 400,000 visitors. However, the sector faces enormous challenges, both at home and abroad. At least four shocks of varying intensity affected the upward trend that started in late 2014: Hurricane Irma (September 2017); travel alerts issued by the US Department of State (mid- and late September 2017); the temporary moratorium on granting licenses in several categories of private business directly connected with tourism (July 2018); and the 2017 and 2019 restrictive measures of the Trump administration. A key question going forward is whether these impacts are temporary or will have a permanent effect on the markets involved.

The year 2018 marked another complex situation for the economy. Cuban authorities estimated economic growth of around 2.2 percent, supported by sectors such as communications, retail, manufacturing, public health, and construction. Decreases were reported in tourism and the sugar industry.

While the government invested only 85 percent of its budgeted goal, these expenditures still represented an almost 15 percent increase over 2017.

A NEW CONSTITUTION

The most important political process in Cuba in 2019 was the public discussion surrounding the new constitution. The new *Magna Carta* proposes transformations in a group of key areas of the country's economic, political, and social life. However, the final form these changes take, and their true scope, will be defined later in the legislative process that will adopt the corresponding laws and in their practical application.

The new Cuban constitution establishes the general lines already agreed upon in the documents approved in the 2016 Seventh Party Congress. Likewise, the popular debate led to the modification of certain aspects of the original version (60 percent of the articles were modified), although most of the adaptations can be considered formal, with a few potentially important ones. Cuba defines itself as a socialist state, with an economy based on social ownership over the main means of production and with "socialist" planning as the main coordination mechanism.

Sovereignty resides in the people, who exercise it through the National Assembly of People's Power as the supreme organ. Likewise, the Communist Party retains its role as the leading political entity, and the only one recognized in the constitution. The direct and secret vote of the people is reserved for the deputies to the Cuban Parliament and for the delegates to the Municipal Assemblies of People's Power. The fundamental executive positions of the state and the government are chosen by these two bodies.

The constitution recognizes a wider variety of individual rights, including the possibility of suing the state and the government for bias, and incorporates the right of habeas corpus. Although there was a modification with respect to the original project, the text opens the door to the recognition of same-sex unions, to be included in a new Family Code that the populace will have to approve. This issue was the most debated in public discussions preceding the referendum on the constitution, according to information provided by the government. The fundamental means of communication can only be owned by the state or political and mass organizations. The interpretation of this article and what it represents for the growing number of independent media that do not have legal recognition will have to wait for the adoption of the corresponding laws.

One of the areas that incorporates significant changes is the organization of Cuba's economic model. Title II includes the so-called Economic Fundamentals, while other rights of this type are included in Title V's "Rights, Duties and Guarantees." In general, Title II follows three basic guidelines.

First, it adheres to the provisions of the so-called Conceptualization of the Cuban economic and social model. Second, although the text makes sure to underline that in Cuba the typical market economy system does not apply, it introduces appreciable transformations that bring the effective model closer to what are known as mixed economies, where different forms of property coexist and there is space for market relations.

For the first time since 1959, the constitution explicitly recognizes private ownership over means of production. This is one of the milestones of the proposal and one of the changes that has the greatest potential to generate future transformations. In addition, the document recognizes and extends the possibility of mixed ownership (i.e., property formed by the combination of two or more forms of ownership, such as a private restaurant and a cooperative farm), which can generate unpredictable dynamics. Likewise, for the first time the market is mentioned as part of the economic and social model. The state also promotes and guarantees foreign investment. Notably, given the recognition of various forms of property in Article 22 and the protections provided for foreign investment in Article 28, the constitution provides private property owned by Cuban nationals with the fewest guarantees, which is a disincentive for investment.

In addition, the text includes the right of workers to participate in the planning, regulation, management, and control of the economy. Language that refers to the concentration of property in non-state subjects was modified with a more neutral tone, and this provision was also extended to entities of this type. Nonetheless, a bias against the private and cooperative sector, especially the former, is maintained.

In many areas the constitution is more modern and flexible than the one dating from 1976. Progress is being made in shaping the economic model and individual rights. However, the essence of the Cuban system remains intact through the economic and political model that it enshrines. A constitution establishes the general framework, but it is up to the Cuban government to develop the new elements contained in the text. After this transcendental political moment, the government can once again focus on the pressing economic problems facing the country. It would seem that circumstances recommend haste more than a pause.

AUSTERITY IS BACK, AGAIN

The economic outlook has darkened, and once-thriving links with many countries in the Western Hemisphere have deteriorated rapidly since the start of 2018.

The reasons for this slowdown include external and domestic aspects. The external economic context changed negatively for Cuba. First, there was the economic crisis in Venezuela, whose effects were felt strongly in foreign trade. That country had been Cuba's first market for medical services and pharmaceuticals, and it was the main supplier of Cuba's oil and derivatives. Between 2014 and 2018, the Venezuelan economy contracted more than 50 percent, according to the International Monetary Fund.[6] Oil production went from 2.5 million barrels per day in 2014 to only 830,000 in April 2019, a contraction of 67 percent.[7]

The drop in oil shipments must have been substantial. Trade figures show that exchanges between the two countries contracted by as much as 57 percent in the period 2014–2018, reflecting both a drop in the oil price and a reduction in supplies. In August 2017, the joint venture ended between Venezuelan state oil firm PDVSA and Cuba's Oil Union CUPET at the refinery in Cienfuegos. That association had enabled Cuba to export oil by-products that had become a significant source of foreign exchange.

In addition, relations with Brazil, which had been Cuba's second-largest trading partner in the region, began to deteriorate in late 2018. In response to President-Elect Jair Bolsonaro's November 2018 demand that Cuba renegotiate the terms of the agreement by which Cuban doctors served mostly poor and remote areas, the Cuban government decided to end its participation in the Mais Médicos program. The participation of Cuban doctors was made possible through a technical cooperation project between the Pan American Health Organization (PAHO), the World Health Organization (WHO), and the Ministries of Health of Brazil and Cuba. In the end Cubans represented almost two-thirds of the total professionals hired. The annual Brazilian transfers to Cuba were estimated to be between $250 million and $300 million. In addition, export guarantees available to Brazilian food producers were suspended, almost halting sales to Cuba. Brazil had enjoyed a significant market share in the island's food purchases since 2004.

A third problem relates to the erratic performance of two of Cuba's main export industries, nickel and sugar, which have been adversely affected by setbacks in production and a decline in world market prices. Nickel production stagnated in the 2014–2018 period after the closing of one of three production plants and operational setbacks in a second one. Prices also declined by 22 percent from 2014 to 2018. Sugar exports earned $180 million in 2018, less than half the amount earned in 2014. Foreign visitors and associated income have been essentially flat since 2017 owing to restrictions in the US market, as well as drops in the Canadian and European markets. The trend has continued into 2019. In June, the number of visitors declined by as much as 20 percent owing essentially to new US sanctions. Overall, Cuba lost more than $4 billion in export revenues in the period. Simultaneously, outflows grew as the island entered new debt-restructuring agreements.

A fourth problem has been the new policies of the US administration, which have had a particularly adverse impact on travel, investment, trade, finance, and remittances.

Following restrictions aimed at curbing travel to Cuba in November 2017, the US administration introduced further measures in April 2019, including a cap on remittances, sanctions on vessels and companies involved in fuel transportation from Venezuela to Cuba, the elimination of the "people-to-people" educational category for authorized travel, the banning of cruise ships from docking in Cuban ports, and stricter enforcement of financial sanctions leading to fines of European banks. The American government also activated the implementation of Title III of the Helms-Burton Act, which had been waived by every administration since the law was enacted in 1996. Under Title III, lawsuits are allowed in US courts against American and foreign companies doing business in Cuba by using property nationalized by the Cuban government following the 1959 Revolution. This more hostile bilateral climate may well have dissuaded both potential investors from third countries and US companies that had an interest in commercial relations with Cuba.

On the domestic front, as discussed earlier, between mid-2015 and mid-2019, hardly any new measures were adopted as part of the *actualización* process. Modifications that entered into force in the latter part of that period can be considered restrictive or of little practical value for the purpose of development.

Cuban authorities have responded to this challenging scenario with a policy mix that combines traditional tools with more unconventional approaches. Since July 2016, strong measures have been adopted to save resources in the public sector, particularly in relation to energy, by reducing physical allocations to state entities. Likewise, import controls have been used to maintain a positive trade balance. By way of illustration, between 2013 and 2018, imports fell by 20 percent, a reduction that could not be attributed solely to price moderation in international markets.

Taking into account the high proportion of intermediate goods in Cuban foreign purchases, which reaches 61 percent, the reduction had a negative effect on domestic production, particularly in the manufacturing industry. Other effects could be seen in retail, which has suffered from recurrent shortages of high-demand products, and with medicines. Meanwhile, the government insisted on maintaining a conservative approach to taking new loans as a way to smooth out the impact of the slowdown. In a certain sense, this decision was understandable given the almost endless cycle of indebtedness that the country is carrying. The government has insisted on fulfilling its international obligations, particularly its sovereign debt. Until October 2018, Cuba duly made the payments corresponding to the agreement with the Paris

Club but was forced to reschedule several commitments with suppliers and foreign investors.

High borrowing costs are linked to domestic issues and the US sanctions. However, it is difficult to imagine how Cuba could restart its productive system without fresh resources to finance investments. A missing piece in this approach is a reasonable strategy to ensure that resources are used appropriately.

The government has also implemented some countercyclical measures. First, the public budget has been used to stimulate the economy. Public spending has grown faster than GDP since 2015. In this context, the fiscal deficit widened from 2.2 percent (of nominal GDP) in 2014 to 8.1 percent in 2018. Fortunately, the pressure on prices is lower, given that this imbalance is now financed mainly by the issuance of public debt, whose participation can reach up to 70 percent of the deficit. However, there could also be negative side effects for the state banks that are buying those bonds.[8] Here it should be noted that the amounts allocated to capital expenditures have increased more rapidly than the total.

Another positive aspect is that the government has continued to prioritize productive investment, which has maintained an upward trajectory, although still far from the necessary amounts. In the period considered, total investments increased by 77 percent, at an annual rate of 15.4 percent, while nominal GDP only increased by 4.5 percent. The structure of investment has also changed positively; during the period these had been directed mainly toward infrastructure, manufacturing, and real estate associated with tourism.

Foreign investment has received growing attention in recent years. A minimal review of the government's economic policy shows that the attraction of foreign investment is practically the only relevant area where there have been no backward steps since the reform was launched. Foreign investment's role is a relatively new phenomenon in the Cuban context. Although it took off during the 1990s, at that time there was a high degree of discretion and gradualism in attracting new companies, which led to the consolidation of a relatively restrictive and selective process. During Havana's 2018 International Trade Fair, it was announced that since March 2014 (when the Foreign Investment Law was adopted), Cuba has signed some 200 new businesses with foreign capital (34 in the Mariel Zone), with a committed capital of $5.5 billion, or a rate of $1.2 billion per year, half of what has been recognized as necessary. In the first half of 2019, new contracts had been signed worth almost $1.3 billion.

However, a much smaller amount has actually been invested, so the impact on economic activity is still modest. Additionally, some of the main contracts are golf courses with associated real-estate development, with weak effects on domestic production capacity.

Table 2.2 Foreign Direct Investment in Cuba

	New Contracts Outside ZEDM*	New Contracts at ZEDM*	Total Amount (millions of USD)
March 2014–June 2019	140	34	6,800
January–June 2019	40	—	1,300

Source: Remarks by the Minister of Foreign Trade and Investment at FIHAV 2018 and Cuba Business Forum, June 2019.
* Mariel Special Development Zone.

The existence of unconventional mechanisms for the allocation of production factors and for the formation of key prices (exchange rates, wages) generates significant distortions in these areas, which are critically important for the decision to penetrate any foreign market. Management of the exchange rate, for example, has a direct impact on the expected return on investment and on the effective ability to repatriate dividends. Up to now, ad hoc solutions have been tested, but these are not the solution to the problem. Once in the field, the foreign investor must deal with a decision-making process whose transparency could be significantly improved, which would help build trust. Decision-making is, in addition, generally dilatory and highly bureaucratic and administrative, which increases the opportunity cost of time and the resources invested. There is still a long way to go in this area, but it is encouraging that some progress has been made.

In December 2018, Cuba started suffering from acute shortages of basic products like wheat flour, eggs, chicken, sausages, cooking oil, powdered milk, and others. Although the situation improved by early June 2019, energy supplies also tightened, with unscheduled blackouts and queues at gas stations in July.

As part of a response to the crisis, the Cuban government announced a set of economic measures meant to address the country's delicate socioeconomic situation. They included a variety of provisions to stimulate exports inclusive of the non-state sector, greater capacity for the management of resources, and more efficient use of the labor force for state enterprises. Notable changes were: a wage increase for workers in social services and administration, the design of alternatives for the productive use of remittances, stricter control over budgets and expenses, and the development of options to retain the outflow of foreign currency associated with individual purchases overseas. Authorities also indicated that the economy would gradually move in a direction based on economic-financial mechanisms, which would replace the administrative guidelines, and they highlighted the role of the financial system and the centrality of exports along with the idea that even greater changes in the planning and management of the economy should be expected.

The decision to improve salaries in the public sector is controversial, amid a decrease in imports and a slowdown in economic activity. Unfortunately, while stressing the need to boost domestic production, the government decided to address inflation concerns by imposing price controls, including in the private and cooperative sectors. It is clear that supply is very inelastic in Cuba due to rigidities and structural factors. The reaction to changes in demand is slow because of a wide range of restrictions, ranging from the functioning of companies to the availability of resources. The nature of domestic production determines that a high proportion of inputs are imported, a feature that will not change in the medium term. The supply could also rise through the importation of final consumer goods, but the current situation in the balance of payments rules out that scenario. In short, the dynamics of supply is determined, to a large extent, by the availability of foreign exchange necessary to purchase imported supplies or consumer goods. While Cuban trade hasn't declined to the catastrophic level of the 1990s, and Cuba's external finances do not indicate the likelihood of such a catastrophe, the near-term forecast is for continued shortages.

Suppressing the action of market mechanisms is counterproductive. Structural measures directed at increasing supply efficiently, not price caps, can provide for sustainable improvements in purchasing capacity and material well-being. If production fails to keep up with demand, and prices cannot adjust accordingly, the path forward will be scarcity, queues, and informal activity. All of these problems are well known by the Cuban population. Moreover, low prices benefit both wealthy and poor people, which enhances inequality. It does not seem consistent with the officials' claim about deploying more financial and economic mechanisms. It remains to be seen how far the other structural measures are taken and to what extent Cuban companies can react to them in a context of a strained financial capacity.

The overall assessment of the current government's response to the economic situation is mixed. On one hand, it is encouraging to see the government reverse some of the most restrictive measures on the *"cuentapropistas"* and somewhat ease obstacles on private business. Likewise, the movement beyond rhetoric with a package of economic measures, some of them structural in nature, offers a ray of hope. However, the arguments advanced by key officials to justify the imposition of price controls, including on the private sector, lack substantial credibility. Protecting the purchasing power of citizens by acting mostly on the price side of the equation is shortsighted.

CONCLUSION

Fulfilling the initial goal of the economic reforms remains a work in progress. The economy has stagnated for at least four years, and the pace of transformation has slowed significantly. Not least, Cuba now faces a more challenging context in the Western Hemisphere than it did ten years ago.

If the reformers hoped to change essential elements of the Cuban economic model, improve economic performance, and increase the standard of living of a majority of Cubans, their plans have not been successful. To achieve better results in the future, the design and implementation of policies has to be professionalized. The ability to retain competent employees in the public sector depends on whether they can improve their living standards and advance in a successful career. The low compensation, rigidity, and hypertrophy of the public sector currently discourages state employees.

The documents that the government has adopted provide an opportunity to begin by laying the basic foundations for reform. But the "actualization" itself suffers from serious internal contradictions.[9] The economic growth that is proclaimed in public discourse is incompatible with the restrictions that weigh on the non-state sector, with the enormous state bureaucracy, the excess of unnecessary control, and the ignorance of basic elements of the functioning of an economic system. Conceiving a dynamic economy where all sectors and social strata advance at the same speed is an illusion. Some degree of inequality is concomitant to dynamic economies. As long as it results from more wealth being created by intrinsically asymmetric industries along key economic dimensions, those income disparities are a reasonable trade-off for more rapid growth in a society that otherwise suffers from not producing enough material progress, and in turn they should not be feared. To make matters worse, Cuba has suffered from a stagnant economy with growing inequality for three decades. Income inequality measured by the Gini Index jumped from 0.24 in 1986 to 0.45 in 2017.[10] In addition, a new social contract could be negotiated to make sure all citizens are guaranteed their basic needs.

Several essential aspects of the model have to be modified so that the aspirations for progress are made concrete. Cuban authorities should not continue the tradition of seeking solutions abroad for the country's domestic problems. New markets for medical services and foreign capital are elements of a strategy that pays off, but they do not replace the work that is required at home.

Attracting additional resources is of little use if there is no reasonable framework within which they can be efficiently invested. In that sense, the current monetary and exchange scheme has to change so that prices reflect the real operating conditions of the economy. And the different agents of the economy must be able to make autonomous decisions on consumption, savings, and investments. Despite policy biases and harsh conditions, Cuba's non-state sector shows maturity. Non-state entities manage 67.5 percent of arable land (they only own 20.7 percent) and produce 88 percent of agricultural output. In Havana, until very recently, private cabs maintained a significant market share, and even though authorities said they were not the backbone of public transportation, residents in the city learned otherwise after December 7, 2018, when many drivers engaged in a work slowdown to protest government regulations. Restaurants are overwhelmingly owned by "*cuentapropistas*," and private "bed-and-breakfast" accommodations account for 33 percent of total stayovers. Locking down these potential sources of growth will be increasingly difficult and economically costly. This area, alongside much-needed reform in the public sector, prominently in state-owned companies, is the key to boosting economic growth.

Going back and forth over the same issues is not a good recipe for success. It should be clear that there is much more than just economic growth at stake.

Chapter Three

Cuban Foreign Policy, 2014–2019

From Raúl Castro to Miguel Díaz-Canel

John M. Kirk

Between 2006 and 2018 Raúl Castro was president of Cuba, both as interim leader for the first two years (while his elder brother was seriously ill), and subsequently as elected president. During that period several conclusions about Cuba's foreign policy can be drawn: in general it followed the internationalist path taken by Fidel Castro since 1959; medical collaboration continued in dozens of developing countries and was the major source of hard currency; China was starting to develop a major political and commercial interest in Cuba; Cuba's regional ties, particularly with ALBA (the Bolivarian Alliance for the Americas) and CELAC (Community of Latin American and Caribbean States), were stronger than ever; and finally, significant steps had been taken to reduce the antagonism between Washington and Havana. To a certain extent some of these trends continued during the 2014–2019 period considered here, while at the same time major challenges started to emerge.

"A week is a long time in politics" is a saying often attributed to British prime minister Harold Wilson—and it is true. Understandably, an analysis of the last five years of Cuban foreign policy therefore affords us a broad sweep of developments, often confusing and at times apparently contradictory. Indeed we have witnessed both new diplomatic opportunities emerging and some reversals in what appeared at the time to be solid alliances. For example, gone from the political scene during this period were longtime allies such as Brazilian president Dilma Rousseff (impeached and removed from office in 2016), Bolivian president Evo Morales (who sought asylum in Argentina), and three-time president Rafael Correa of Ecuador (who left office in 2017 only to see his dreams of "socialism of the twenty-first century" postponed after former vice president Lenín Moreno assumed power and became a vocal critic of his former leader). The most significant change could be found in Venezuela, where severe polarization led to the contested electoral victory of Nicolás Maduro in 2018, followed by political turmoil, economic crisis, and international pressure (discussed later). These were major blows for Cuba's diplomatic ties to formerly steadfast allies and ideological partners in what was known as the "Pink Tide" of socialist and social democratic countries in Latin America.

On the other side of the ledger Cuba's medical internationalism continued (albeit to a noticeably reduced degree), with medical personnel serving around the world—38,262 in sixty-six countries in mid-2018, and "some 30,000" by the end of the year.[1] Meanwhile Cuba's commercial ties with China were in the ascendancy, and Russia was quickly moving to reestablish its own connections with Havana. (This can be seen in the arrival in port of Russian intelligence ship *Viktor Leonov* in January 2015, the day before the visit to Cuba of the most prestigious US diplomatic delegation in thirty-five years to advance the normalization of relations between Havana and Washington.) The strengthening of Cuba's ties with both China and Russia has grown steadily, particularly since the deterioration in relations between Washington and Havana during the Trump administration (2017–present).

Caught in the midst of these changes in foreign policy relations was the complex (and traditionally dysfunctional) relationship between Havana and Washington, which has witnessed some particularly dramatic events in recent years. Chief among these were the simultaneous TV broadcasts on December 17, 2014, by Presidents Barack Obama and Raúl Castro, announcing that they were moving to reopen diplomatic relations (broken by Washington in January 1961). A flurry of announcements followed over the next two years, with the actual embassy buildings being officially reopened in July 2015—a remarkable achievement given decades of enmity. Several key aspects of the innovative approach introduced by Obama were then overturned by the election of Donald Trump, who in June 2017 made his position clear. Speaking in Miami, he declared: "I am canceling the last administration's completely one-sided deal with Cuba."[2] Recent events in the bilateral relationship have diverged radically from the promising events of 2014–2015, as a roller coaster of diplomatic tensions has steadily replaced a policy of incipient rapprochement.

This chapter seeks to summarize these and other foreign policy developments, and to explain the evolution of Cuba's international relations since 2014. There are four major areas that have seen significant change in Cuban foreign policy between 2014 and 2018—Cuba's relations with the European Union, the Global South, international powers Russia and China, and the United States.

CUBA-EUROPEAN RELATIONS

Cuba's relationship with the European Union (EU) had been troubled since 1996, when the EU introduced the Common Position on Cuba, largely as a result of lobbying by Spanish prime minister José María Aznar, and supported by Washington. The objective was quite simply to unite European countries' positions on Cuba into one united front, pressuring Cuba to adapt political reform and human rights targets as set out by the EU. This, it was believed in Brussels, would bring about significant political change in Cuba, resulting in a transition to liberal democracy, greater respect for civil and political human rights, and an improvement in living standards for Cubans. The strategy was a failure. While some of the former socialist allies of Cuba in the EU (most notably Poland, Hungary, and the Czech Republic) adopted a strict policy of seeking to isolate Havana, other members, such as France, Italy, and the United Kingdom, did not.

As a result, the Common Position was anything but common. Even under the Aznar government (1996–2004) the official policy was never fully implemented. Spanish tourist companies (in particular, the Meliá and Iberostar hotel chains) made significant investments in the tourist sector, while Spanish companies continued exporting a variety of goods to the island. Indeed, despite the official rhetoric of European governments, Cuba's major trading partnerships were with EU countries. Meanwhile tourists from European countries continued to visit Cuba in increasing numbers, again revealing the hollow impact of the official EU stance. Put simply, tourism and trade quickly trumped political rhetoric.

The Common Position remained in effect from 1996 to 2016. As early as 2008, however—when the EU launched a political dialogue with Cuba and reintroduced a limited cooperation program—it was obvious that the time had arrived to adopt a fresh approach. In 2014 the EU initiated a process known as the Negotiations for the Political Dialogue and Cooperation Agreement with the island. The new approach recognized that the strategy to isolate Cuba had failed. Instead, political dialogue, improved bilateral cooperation, and greater commercial ties were the new objectives.[3] Slowly but surely the EU position moved toward a pragmatic fence-mending position with Havana, with a series of constructive confidence-building measures steadily introduced. For its part, the Cuban government showed its disposition to accommodate the fresh initiatives, and a constructive dialogue resulted.

For several years there had been clear indications that both sides wanted to improve relations, in no small degree because of the significant trade between the EU and Cuba. In 2016, for instance, the export of EU goods to Cuba was worth 2.04 billion euros, with imports from Cuba totaling 0.41 billion euros.[4] The EU is now the principal foreign investor, the major exporter, and second trade partner of Cuba. Moreover, all twenty-eight members of the EU maintained diplomatic relations with Havana, notwithstanding the umbrella agreement and theoretical objective of regime change that had traditionally been reflected in the Common Position. Indeed, as early as 2003 the EU had established a representative office in Havana, which it upgraded to become an official EU delegation in 2008 and kept open as a means of strengthening diplomatic ties. Confusion and inconsistency had been the hallmarks of the Common Position, and many in the EU were ready to move to a more relevant, updated relationship with Cuba.

After two years of negotiations and high-level exchanges, Cuba and the EU signed an agreement reflecting the changed position in December 2016, which was subsequently ratified by the European Parliament in July 2017. In many ways the 180-degree shift in Cuba's diplomatic relationship with the EU is illustrative of the pragmatic approach in foreign affairs employed by Raúl Castro and continued by his successor, Miguel Díaz-Canel. For its part, the EU came to realize that it lacked the influence to pressure Cuba into making any of what it considered meaningful reforms. Continuity and change, with a healthy dose of economic pragmatism and a reduction of ideology, now made up the essence of Cuban foreign policy—and a strengthened relationship with the EU resulted.

This can be illustrated by the visit of Spanish president Pedro Sánchez in November 2018, the first official visit by somebody of this rank in thirty-two years. The following year saw a flurry of activity as Madrid strongly voiced its political and diplomatic support for Spanish investors in the face of legal threats posed by the application of the Helms-Burton Act. This would allow lawsuits in US courts to be launched against anybody profiting from properties previously owned by American individuals or companies that had been nationalized by the Cuban government in the early years of the Cuban Revolution. For its part Cuba has continued to strengthen its ties with the European Union, participating in several sessions to discuss the official bilateral Political Dialogue and Cooperation Agreement. Newly elected president Miguel Díaz-Canel visited Europe in 2018, meeting with key policy-makers in France and the United Kingdom.

Both Cuba and the EU have worked hard to improve bilateral relations in recent years, and there have been several meetings in both Brussels and Havana between Cuban foreign minister Bruno Rodríguez and his counterpart in the European Union, Federica Mogherini. Economic assistance to Cuba and political dialogue have traditionally been the principal topics, while more recently there has been greater interest in an exchange of views on the troubled Venezuelan situation. Of particular importance was the decision in 2019 by the Trump administration to end the suspension of Title III of the Helms-Burton Act (discussed later in this chapter). European companies were immediately threatened by the legislation, and in fact legal challenges were initiated against some long-standing investors in Cuba. The EU was adamantly opposed to the Helms-Burton Act, as can be seen from a press release issued by the European Union on May 24, 2019, following a meeting of EU and Cuban diplomats: "The decision of the United States to end the suspension of Title III of the Helms-Burton Act was also on the agenda. Regretting the U.S. decision, both the EU and Cuba believe the extraterritorial application of the Act is contrary to international law."[5] It can thus be argued that this policy of the Trump administration actually strengthened Cuban–European Union relations.

A telling symbol of the strengthening relations between Cuba and Europe can be found in the four-day visit to Cuba in March 2019 of Great Britain's Prince Charles and his wife Camilla, Duchess of Cornwall—significantly the first by any member of the UK's royal family. This resulted from a courtesy call made to Prince Charles in London by Cuban president Díaz-Canel in November of 2018. In Cuba the royal couple engaged in various activities: laying a wreath at the statue of Cuba's national hero of the independence movement, José Martí; attending an official dinner hosted by Díaz-Canel; driving a 1953 MG sports car to an antique car rally; having a photograph taken next to the iconic statue of John Lennon; meeting Cuban boxers at a local gym; touring the colonial quarter of Old Havana; meeting with members of the Buena Vista Social Club; and visiting green energy projects. The visit was added at the request of the UK government to a tour of several Commonwealth countries—Barbados, St. Kitts and Nevis, Grenada, St. Lucia, and St. Vincent and the Grenadines—and was intended to both strengthen the potential for enhanced British trade and investment, and take advantage of an incipient opening of the Cuban economy. Some 200,000 British tourists visit Cuba annually, and investment there is slowly increasing. BBC correspondent Nicholas Wichell praised the initiative shown by the British government and summed up the royal visit by noting that the visit "showed the UK in a 'strikingly different' position to the U.S."[6]

Cuba's Ties with the Developing World

Internationalism

Throughout the years that Fidel Castro was the leader of Cuba he emphasized the need for developing ties with the Global South. This commitment was multifaceted and consistently emphasized the importance of socioeconomic collaboration with countries in Africa, Asia, and in particular Latin America. The preamble of the 2019 Cuban constitution, for example, mentions the need to support "proletarian internationalism . . . fraternal friendship, the help, cooperation, and solidarity of the peoples of the world, especially those of Latin America and the Caribbean."[7] For decades Cuba's soft power role in developing countries has been extraordinary, providing numerous benefits for the recipient countries while also affording Cuba widespread support in international fora.[8]

Cuba's support for developing countries started with the advent of the revolutionary government in 1959 and continues to this day. Its role is sui generis and extremely wide-ranging, and while Cuba has a population of only 11.2 million people, its profile in the Global South is significant.[9] As one observer noted about Havana's role in Africa, for example, "Cuba was the only economically underdeveloped state which carried out, effectively, an African policy comparable to that of great powers . . . the Cuban role in Africa was unprecedented."[10] Cuba's presence there is notable, with thirty-one embassies (while twenty-six African countries have embassies on the island). Cuba's medical cooperation, particularly in sub-Saharan Africa, is also exceptional, while its collaborative role in a variety of spheres ranging from education to engineering, culture to biotechnology, is well recognized and appreciated. Cuba also maintains an active policy of sending politicians abroad to strengthen bilateral ties, and in March 2019 Salvador Valdés Mesa, first vice president of the Councils of State and Ministers, visited Angola and Namibia. He also traveled to South Africa in May 2019 to attend the swearing in of Cyril Ramaphosa, with additional visits to Eswatini (formerly Swaziland), and finally to Ethiopia—where some five thousand students had attended university in Cuba. In addition, Inés María Chapman, another of Cuba's vice presidents, represented Cuba in March 2019 at a meeting of the Southern Africa Development Community held in Pretoria. At the meeting it was announced that 2,046 students from the region had graduated from Cuban universities. In addition to greeting South African leaders, she also met with the presidents of Namibia, Zimbabwe, Uganda, and the Sahrawi Arab Democratic Republic; the prime minister of Lesotho; the vice presidents of Angola and Seychelles; and the foreign minister of Namibia. As can be seen, Cuba maintains a policy of providing substantial development collaboration (the Cubans prefer this to the concept of "aid," which they see as demeaning) while developing diplomatic connections through substantial delegations abroad and invitations to leaders to visit Cuba.

In Latin America, Cuba has seen a strategic deterioration in its relations with several countries in recent years as leftist governments have been voted out. Havana had actively supported the founding of the Community of Latin American and Caribbean States (CELAC), whose second summit took place in Havana in 2014. In 2015, President Raúl Castro attended the VII Summit of the Americas, the first time that a Cuban president had done so. In addition, Cuba had a major role to play in attempting to end the decades-long Colombian civil war, and helped to broker a deal between the Revolutionary Armed Forces of Colombia (or FARC) and the Colombian government.[11]

This was an enormously significant development, following decades of civil war.

While the potential for the consolidation of power by leftist governments in Latin America looked promising in 2014, by 2018 the bloom was off the rose. In particular the election of right-wing governments in Argentina, Brazil, Colombia, and Chile, combined with the decrease in support for CELAC and increasing political tensions in Venezuela, resulted in a disintegration of the block of progressive Latin American governments. Cuba's hasty withdrawal of over eight thousand medical personnel from Brazil following outspoken attacks by President-Elect Jair Bolsonaro illustrates well how the geopolitical tides were turning in Latin America. Moreover, in Colombia the Duque government was clearly not in favor of extending the peace accord with the ELN guerrilla army, and indeed the future of its agreement with the FARC—so laboriously worked out in Havana under President Santos between 2012 and 2016—is unclear. In addition, the inevitable decline in the influence of the ten-country Bolivarian alliance (ALBA in the Spanish acronym) has significantly reduced Cuba's influence with the members. The Pink Tide, composed of socialist and social democratic governments, has now been replaced by a Blue Wave of staunchly conservative governments—and as a result Cuba's influence has waned noticeably.

Cuba still maintains formal diplomatic relations with all the countries of Latin America. That said, there have been serious differences of opinion with both the Organization of American States (OAS, from which Cuba was suspended in 1962) and many individual countries. This is seen most clearly in the opposition to the Cuban position over Venezuela by the members of the Lima Group, a collection of Latin American countries and Canada, including Argentina, Brazil, Chile, Colombia, Costa Rica, Guatemala, Honduras, Panama, Paraguay, and Peru. This group sought the overthrow of the Maduro government and consistently supported the opposition led by Juan Guaidó. Speaking in April 2019, Cuban president Díaz-Canel condemned this alliance: "The Group of Lima once again reiterated its interventionist goals against the Government of Venezuela, and also indicated an alleged negative role of Cuba. Once again they follow the perverse instructions of the United States. Our response is Dignity against the Monroe Doctrine; We are Cuba."[12] While maintaining diplomatic ties and commercial exchange, it is clear that there are now significant differences of opinion between Cuba and some conservative governments in the region, differences that have been seen most clearly over how to deal with the challenges faced in present-day Venezuela.

Cuba's position of support for Nicolás Maduro's government, one of the few leftist governments that remain in Latin America, has also been attacked by the secretary-general of the OAS, Uruguayan Luis Almagro. Since its suspension from the OAS in 1962, Cuba has never been interested in returning to the organization, even after the suspension was lifted conditionally in 2009. From the perspective of Havana, the OAS is seen as being too closely linked with US goals in the region.[13] On the other hand, for Almagro the role of Cuba in Venezuela is extremely negative. If peace is ever to return to Venezuela, he announced, "it will depend essentially upon the pressure that the United States places on two fundamental factors that are oppressing the Venezuelan people: the Cuba factor and the Maduro dictatorship."[14] Cuba has consistently defended the Maduro administration (which it sees as the legitimate government), while opposing the Lima Group (which it sees as a stalking horse for US economic interests, particularly in the petroleum sector).

Despite significant political differences, however, Cuba maintains solid diplomatic relations with most countries in the region, as witnessed by the visits to Cuba in 2018 of the presidents of Venezuela, Bolivia, Panama, El Salvador, Haiti, Suriname, and Guyana, as well as by the prime ministers of Saint Vincent and the Grenadines, Dominica, and Belize. Relations have also increased with Mexico, although it remains to be seen what role the government of Andrés Manuel López Obrador in Mexico will play in the region and to what degree it will support a role for Cuba. To date, the Mexican government seems focused on domestic priorities, and López Obrador has not made clear Mexico's international priorities.

Cuba-Venezuela Relations

In terms of commercial and strategic ties, no bilateral relationship for Cuba has been more important over the past eighteen years than its connection with Venezuela. Throughout the presidency of Hugo Chávez (1999–2013) the two countries developed a symbiotic relationship, forming increasingly strong bonds in terms of economic and social programs (particularly in health care and education), but also establishing military and intelligence connections, as well as dozens of joint economic ventures. These extremely close ties continue, albeit without the impact of the earlier Fidel Castro–Chávez ties, and no country has supported Maduro more than Cuba.

Chávez saw himself (and was seen by many) as the "spiritual son" of Fidel Castro in many ways. Together the two countries created scores of bilateral development projects, and Havana sent tens of thousands of Cubans to Venezuela on collaboration missions, mainly in the fields of health care and education. Meanwhile Venezuela became the island's major trading partner and kept Cuba's economy ticking by selling billions of barrels of oil at below market rates in exchange for educational and in particular medical assistance. The death of Chávez, following months of medical treatment in Havana, was a major blow for Venezuela and ultimately affected the bilateral relationship. That said, both countries needed each other, for ongoing diplomatic, commercial, and ideological reasons, and both have maintained close bilateral ties since the death of Chávez in March 2013. Moreover, despite an economy in ruins and the departure of an estimated three million Venezuelans fleeing runaway inflation, hunger, and a polarized country, the Bolivarian Republic of Venezuela has remained Cuba's most consistent ally. No longer, though, was it Havana's major trading partner—a position taken up by China. Relations in political, diplomatic, and strategic matters remained firm, as symbolized by the visit to Havana in April 2018 of President Nicolás Maduro, the first foreign leader to meet newly elected President Miguel Díaz-Canel. The Cuban president remains in close contact with his Venezuelan counterpart, and in a visit to Caracas in late July of 2019 he emphasized his "unconditional support for Venezuela and the Bolivarian Revolution" while condemning the "imperialist plans against a besieged Venezuela."[15]

There is no doubt, however, that bilateral ties have been weakened because of the major problems facing the Venezuelan economy. Oil, the country's primary export, sold for $142 per barrel in 2008 but had plummeted to $56 per barrel in mid-2019, and obviously this has had a major impact on the shared goals and development plans laid out in 2000 by Fidel Castro and Hugo Chávez. At its peak, tens of thousands of Cuban medical personnel arrived to bolster the poor health care system in Venezuela, while in return Chávez provided heavily subsidized fuel to Cuba. This came at a time when the prices for oil were high in the world market and the Venezuelan economy prospered, but as the price of oil declined, domestic Venezuelan opposition to the arrangement grew. In terms of bilateral trade, the data are quite stark. In 2012 crude and refined oil exports to Cuba represented a total of 104,000 barrels per day (bpd)—roughly 60 percent of Cuba's total oil supply.[16] At that time there were some forty thousand Cuban professionals in Venezuela, 75 percent of whom were medical professionals. Overall bilateral trade with Venezuela at the time accounted for 21 percent of Cuba's GDP, and the two countries had an extremely close ideological, commercial, and strategic relationship.

Chávez's death marked the beginning of a major decrease in trade. Ideological and strategic relations remained strong, with multiple government delegations flying constantly between Caracas and Havana. But as oil prices fell precipitously, trade suffered badly—from $7.3 billion in 2014 to $2.2 billion in 2017.[17] Cuba received 103,226 bpd in the first half of 2015, but this had fallen to 72,350 bpd during the same period in 2017. Irregular supplies continued in 2018, accentuated by policies of the Trump administration to disrupt Venezuelan oil exports—currently an estimated 40,000 bpd. As a result of the major decrease in oil supplies from Venezuela, Havana started to increase fuel purchases from Russia (which has also started to drill for oil on the island). In January 2018, Cuba also signed a three-year agreement with Algeria for oil. The impact on Cuban society has been noticeable, since fuel allocations to government offices were cut 28 percent in 2018, and public lighting reduced 50 percent. Venezuela remains a strong ally, but its disastrous economic situation has resulted in severely weakened commercial ties, a situation that has led Cuba to seek other strategic alliances for essential supplies and trade.

While commercial relations have suffered, largely because of Venezuela's disastrous economic situation, diplomatic relations remain strong. Both Cuba and Venezuela, along with Nicaragua, constitute the vestiges of leftist governments from earlier times. Their ideological roots are profoundly intertwined, as are commercial ties—with an arrangement of bartering petroleum for medical assistance continuing, albeit in reduced format.

International Cooperation

Cuba's collaboration with developing countries is exceptional. Consider that Cuba has more medical personnel working in Third World countries than all industrialized countries combined. During the period from 2014 to 2018, and indeed since Raúl Castro took over power from his brother, first on a temporary basis between 2006 and 2008 and then as president until 2018, there has also been a pattern of continuity and change in terms of Cuban international collaboration. In general terms, however, it can be stated that, unlike Fidel Castro, his younger brother was more strategic in supporting Cuban internationalist efforts. As a result, collaboration with the Global South has continued, but is now applied in a more selective approach.

Cuba's policy of educational cooperation and medical internationalism has provided excellent examples of this application of foreign policy, although the approach has significantly evolved in recent years. For instance, in July 2016 there were an estimated 55,000 Cuban medical professionals working in 67 countries,[18] while three years later this had dropped to some 30,000. Why the sudden decrease? In essence it comes down to politics and economics. Venezuela had for many years been the major recipient of Cuban medical cooperation, paying for these services (as well as education, military, and intelligence support) with fuel. Caracas had also been the major financier of Cuban medical internationalism programs throughout the region. As noted above, the significant decrease in oil supplies has resulted in a downsizing of Cuban cooperation with Venezuela. Medical cooperation does continue with Venezuela but has been scaled back.

The next-largest source of medical cooperation had been with Brazil, but after the government of Dilma Rousseff was replaced by the right-wing administration of Michel Temer in 2016, there was a decrease in the number of physicians working there in the Mais Médicos program—from some 11,000 in 2015 to 8,600 in late 2017. In November 2018, Cuba closed its medical program in Brazil in response to demands by President-Elect Bolsonaro that Cuban doctors go through an arduous relicensing process, and that they receive 100 percent of the payments Brazil gives to Cuba for their services. (Prior to this time, Cuban medical personnel received approximately $1,100 monthly, with the remaining $3,000 paid by the Brazilian government being directed to the Cuban government, ostensibly to support the Cuban health care service.) Closing the program has resulted in a loss of approximately $400 million annually for the Cuban government. More significant, however, was the decrease in income generated by medical services in Venezuela. The Chávez government had subsidized much of Cuba's medical internationalism work—in particular the "Operation Miracle" ophthalmology program that had provided over four million free eye surgeries in thirty-four countries.[19] Because of the dire economic circumstances in Venezuela, this financial support has been greatly reduced, resulting in Cuba becoming more pragmatic in its medical internationalism program. The number of countries receiving Cuban medical collaboration remains approximately the same, but the number of participants working there has fallen significantly.

Even before these political developments had made an impact upon Cuban cooperation, however, it was obvious that Raúl Castro preferred to amend the traditional Cuban approach that his brother had developed over the decades. In April 2011, the government published the "Resolution on the Guidelines of the Economic and Social Policy of the Party and the Revolution," a process which had been designed to provide a national discussion on Cuban economic reality, and ultimately to update it so as to better serve the Cuban people. Economic pragmatism, rather than socialist ideology, now came to the fore and, while humanitarian goals were still extremely important for Cuba, it was also clear that the country could not afford the magnanimous gestures of the past that had been the hallmark of Fidel Castro's foreign policy.

An example of the earlier approach to emergency medical collaboration can be seen in Cuba's response to the 2005 earthquake that hit the Kashmir region of Pakistan, killing almost 100,000 people. It is worth noting that these programs were provided at no charge to the affected regions. Within days, Cuba sent more than 2,500 medical personnel, establishing 32 field hospitals (later donated to Pakistan), treating at no cost over a million patients, delivering tons of medicines and equipment, and subsequently providing 1,000 scholarships to train Pakistani medical students in Cuba. Likewise, after the disastrous meltdown of the Chernobyl nuclear plant in Ukraine in 1986, the Cuban government provided treatment in Havana for over 26,000 victims of radiation (including 22,000 children from Ukraine). The program was discontinued in 2011, after the Ukrainian government failed to meet its commitment to initiate financial support. In May of 2019, however, about fifty Ukrainian children returned to Cuba under the auspices of the charitable organization Bogoluobov's International Charitable Foundation for Life. It is instructive to compare the example of the massive humanitarian aid that Fidel Castro initiated in 1990 (precisely at a time when the Cuban economy was in dire straits because of the implosion of the Soviet Union) with the new, significantly reduced approach established under Raúl Castro and continued under Díaz-Canel.

This can also be seen clearly in the response to the leading role of Cuba in the 2014 campaign against Ebola in West Africa (with the participation of over 250 medical personnel), compared with its absence in the renewed outbreak of 2018–2019. The medical internationalism heroics of a decade ago have been replaced by severely reduced offerings, as seen, for example, in the contribution of a delegation of forty medical personnel sent to Mozambique in the wake of massive flooding in 2019. It remains to be seen if the World Health Organization will again invite the collaboration of Cuban medics to deal with the new Ebola outbreak, but so far the lack of Cuban involvement has been noticeable.

Articles 111 and 112 of the 2011 Guidelines designed to establish economic priorities in Cuba made very clear this new direction of Cuban cooperation. The document was notably cautious about the cost of such missions. It recommended, "where practical, consider a payment requirement to cover at least the costs incurred by Cuba in its solidarity cooperation projects." Article 112 also indicated the need for fiscal prudence, encouraging government planners to "promote multilateral cooperation, particularly with UN agencies, as a way to obtain financial resources and technologies in keeping with Cuba's national development priorities."[20] Generous, unquestioning medical support was now subject to detailed cost analysis.

This is not to say that Cuba has stopped providing medical assistance where it is needed, but rather that it has become more selective in the type of medical collaboration that it offers. Cuba also provides other forms of medical support.[21] A sliding scale of payment has gradually been introduced into these various collaboration programs. Countries with extremely limited resources (such as the many sub-Saharan countries where Cuban doctors work, or Haiti) pay very little for medical assistance. By contrast there is a sizeable Cuban medical presence in the Middle East—such as Qatar, where there are some five hundred Cuban medical professionals working in Dukhan—and oil-rich countries pay significantly more for services. Likewise, medical students from poor countries pay nothing for their medical training at the Latin American Medical School, whereas those from wealthier countries contribute to their medical education.

In sum, in recent years Cuba has decided to exploit more rationally its greatest source of fund generation—its human capital. This has been pursued while respecting humanitarian goals and yet insisting that, whenever possible, payment be made for services rendered. In most cases, payment is significantly below generally accepted international rates, yet it still provides income to the Cuban state—an estimated $7 billion annually for medical services. This approach governs missions sent abroad, as well as educational programs and, increasingly, medical tourism services offered to foreigners.

Great Power Relations

China

In 1960, Cuba established diplomatic relations with China, at that time the only country in the Western Hemisphere to do so. While bilateral relations have waxed and waned since then, the two countries have increased trade, and China has become a key political ally of Cuba. China became the major trading partner of Cuba in 2016, with bilateral trade of $2.58 billion, compared to $2.24 billion for Venezuela.[22] In addition, in 2011 China canceled a large part of Cuba's $6 billion debt to Beijing.[23] This increasing interest in Cuba is a significant aspect of a detailed Chinese policy to expand its political and commercial influence throughout Latin America. Beijing views Cuba as both a safe ideological ally as well as a springboard from which to launch commercial and strategic ventures in Latin America and the Caribbean.

In terms of trade, Chinese goods can be found throughout the island. Tourists rent Geely cars and are transported to their resorts in Yutong buses. Meanwhile Cuban consumers use Haier domestic appliances and Huawei electronic equipment, construction companies use Sinotruks to transport supplies, Chinese rolling stock is increasingly found on Cuban railway tracks, and farmers drive YTO tractors. Moreover, investment projects have finally started to grow after a sluggish start. Cuba has joint venture agreements in biotechnology and health care (with processing plants in both countries), while China has provided support for a container terminal in Santiago de Cuba and cranes for the port of Mariel outside Havana, and is investing in renewable energy as well as computer assembly projects. This is a remarkable development in recent years.

China also has taken an interest in Cuba's tourist industry, and Air China has been operating in Cuba since 2015. There are now flights from Shanghai to Havana, with a brief stopover in Montreal. Almost all of the buses used by tourists on the island are from China, as are 65 percent of the rental cars, while Chinese investment has also allegedly contributed to a $500 million golf resort under development east of Havana. The number of Chinese tourists also continues to increase—some fifty thousand in 2018. While not overly startling, these developments show an increased interest on the part of Beijing in developing new, closer commercial ties with Cuba.

On other fronts, China donated $36 million to various development projects in 2018. These range from port modernization to a livestock recovery

program, solar energy to water system infrastructure. In addition, China donated $7.7 million in rice for public consumption, and has also provided
hurricane relief, as well as rescheduling debts following natural disasters on
the island. These are all recent developments, and they illustrate the growing
interest in Cuba by Beijing.

Bilateral political ties also continue to strengthen. In 2014 President Xi
Jinping visited Cuba, followed by Vice-Premier Li Keqiang in 2015 and
Premier Li Keqiang in 2016—the first by a Chinese premier to Cuba since
diplomatic relations were established in 1960. He met with Fidel Castro
during the visit and signed some thirty economic cooperation agreements. In
2017, trade union leader Li Yufu held meetings with his Cuban counterpart,
while the leader of Cuba's National Assembly, Esteban Lazo, led a parlia-
mentary delegation to China that year. Significantly, the prestigious 2018
Havana Book Fair was dedicated to China. Finally, in November 2018 President Miguel Díaz-Canel met with the Chinese president and prime minister
during his state visit to Beijing, his first major trip abroad since becoming
president. (On that mission he also visited Russia, North Korea, Vietnam,
and Laos, with a working visit while in transit to France and the United
Kingdom.) Speaking in China, Díaz-Canel made clear the difference in policy that Beijing and Washington had toward Cuba: "Looking at both the past
and future China is opening doors while others build walls."[24]

As can be seen, several key aspects of the relationship between Havana
and Beijing have grown apace during the period under study. Following a
visit to China in May 2019, Cuban foreign minister Bruno Rodríguez noted
that China and countries of the Global South were "natural allies." Cuba
would continue to demonstrate solidarity with Beijing, and he added that the
"historic, traditional ties between China and Cuba were at their highest moment."[25] Cuba also agreed to participate in several commercial initiatives of
the Chinese government, including the innovative Belt and Road project—a
global development strategy of Beijing that concentrates on infrastructure
development and investment. The diplomatic opening established by the Obama administration served as a catalyst for Chinese commercial interest in
the region, resulting in two schools of thought to explain this recent development. For some, the US interest meant that it was safe for Chinese business
people to invest in Cuba, while for others it was based upon the need to take
a leading role in Cuba before US companies seized the initiative. For the
Chinese government, geostrategic interests have also played a significant
role as China seeks to establish political alliances in the Global South.

Russia

Just as China has sought to take advantage of the isolationist stance of the
Trump administration and strengthen its ties with Cuba, so too has Russia

pursued a similar policy of filling the political and commercial vacuum since 2017. Following the implosion of the Soviet Union three decades ago, bilateral ties with Russia waned significantly, and for several years Cuba was studiously neglected in Moscow government circles. But in recent years the relationship with Havana has been revived and strengthened, driven largely by Cuba's commercial needs and Russia's geopolitical interests. This swiftly evolving relationship can be seen in Russian president Vladimir Putin's visit to Havana in July 2014, and those of Raúl Castro to Moscow in May 2015 and Miguel Díaz-Canel in November 2018. Foreign Minister Bruno Rodríguez followed up this initiative in March 2019, and in meetings with his counterpart Sergei Lavrov discussed closer economic ties, as well as the appropriate policy to support the Maduro government in Venezuela. Lavrov also emphasized Moscow's firm opposition to US policy toward the island: "We share with our Cuban friends a condemnation of the illegal pressure that results from sanctions, and reiterate the categorical rejection of the economic, commercial and financial blockade of Cuba maintained by the United States. We will continue to support firmly the just demands of Havana about the immediate end of that blockade."[26] In July 2019 Lavrov flew to Havana to continue discussions about shared foreign policy goals and growing commercial ties. His message about strengthening ties with Cuba was clear: "Our policy towards Cuba is that we shall support Cuba's people not only politically, not only morally, not only by means of developing military technical cooperation but also by encouraging trade and economic projects to help that country's economy become more resistant to all kinds of external threats."[27]

The resurgence of Russian interest in Cuba in recent years is indicated by the 70 percent increase in trade in 2017 over the previous year, with bilateral trade reaching $400 million by late 2018, up from $223 million in 2016 and $187 million in 2015. While this still pales in comparison with Cuba's bilateral trade with China and Venezuela, it suggests a clear intention on the part of both countries to strengthen commercial ties. Chinese goods and services accounted for 22 percent of Cuba's imports in 2017, followed by Spain (14 percent) and Russia (5 percent),[28] while Cuba's major export partners for 2017 were Venezuela (17.8 percent), Spain (14 percent), and Russia (5 percent).[29] In addition there are some thirty Russian companies with offices in Cuba. Illustrative, too, of Moscow's growing interest in Cuba is the increase in the number of Russian tourists who visited the island in 2016—some 65,000. In 2018 some 137,000 Russians came to Cuba, and figures for the January–June period of 2019 showed that 76,000 had already arrived, an increase of 13 percent over the same period in 2018.[30] In recent years Cuba has updated its fleet of airplanes with Russian-built Tupolev, Antonov, and Ilyushin aircraft, and Russia has stated its intention to invest in the notoriously poor Cuban rail service.[31]

The renaissance of Cuba-Russia relations can be traced back to the 2000 visit of Vladimir Putin to Cuba. This resulted in an increased number of trade deals and was followed by Raúl Castro's visit to Moscow in 2009. In 2013 Prime Minister Medvedev traveled to Havana, where he signed several cooperation agreements. This prepared the groundwork for the 2014 visit of Putin to Havana, at which time he forgave some $30 billion of debt accrued during the Soviet-Cuba era, with the remaining $4 billion debt to be invested in various infrastructure projects. Since then, bilateral investment ties have flourished. In May 2017, for example, Roseneft (the Russian state oil company) began sending fuel to Cuba—as supplies from Venezuela faltered. This was the first time this century that Russian fuel had been sent to the island. In January 2017, Roseneft and Cuba's national oil company (CUPET) signed an agreement to develop oil production off the coast of Varadero. The Russian company is also involved in a plan to modernize the Cienfuegos oil refinery.

These developments followed a general agreement signed by Russian minister of foreign affairs Sergey Lavrov and his Cuban counterpart, Bruno Rodríguez, which laid out plans for closer cooperation in international and bilateral matters. This has come in several areas, with growing Russian involvement in the energy, railroad, food production, textile, automobile, and biotechnology areas. Cuba, for instance, ordered locomotives worth $190 million from the Russian company Sinara, and negotiations have taken place with state-run Russian Railways (RZD) for a $2 billion contract to upgrade the Cuban railroad system. Some 2,500 vehicles have been shipped to Cuba by KAMAZ, and in early 2018 over 300 Lada cars arrived in Havana.

Perhaps of greater concern from Washington's perspective are the increasing ties between the Russian and Cuban military. In 2016, Moscow agreed to provide military advice and modernize Cuban military equipment from the Soviet era—although this did not apparently involve the sale of modern weaponry. In late 2018 it agreed to provide a $50 million loan to Cuba for the purchase of Russian military equipment, and an additional $250 million credit to strengthen infrastructure on the island. Significantly, Presidents Putin and Díaz-Canel stated in November 2018—during a visit to Moscow by the Cuban leader—that the two countries had agreed for the present not to reopen two Russian military bases (one for signals detection and the other for naval support) but did not deny that both bases were still possible future projects.[32] In July 2019 Ricardo Cabrisas, vice president of the Council of Ministers, made his third trip of the year to Moscow, where he met with the Russian minister of defense, General Sergey Shoygu, to discuss bilateral cooperation and security issues in the Caribbean. Clearly geostrategic interests and trade have become inextricably linked for both countries.

What can be deduced from these various developments is that Havana and Moscow have steadily developed an important strategic partnership in diplomatic, commercial, and military matters, much along the lines of the ties that have been developed in recent years with China (although with the latter country there are few military ties to date). A resurgence of Russian interest in Cuba has been built on deep, established historical ties, with converging interests of both Cuba and Russia. As Venezuela's economic troubles increase, Havana has needed to broaden its commercial (and in particular energy-related) alternatives. For its part, Russia may well view Cuba once again as a useful ally in gaining a foothold in Latin America. Planned visits in late 2019 of Valentina Matviyenko, chair of the Federation Council, and of Prime Minister Medvedev illustrate the continued interest in strengthening bilateral ties. Of particular note is the growing similarity in foreign policy positions noted by both governments. This is seen most clearly in condemnation of US foreign policy around the globe, and in particular the US attempt to bring about regime change in Venezuela—an issue in which Havana and Moscow have been extremely outspoken and have worked together to oppose.

Both China and Russia share an interest in strengthening bilateral ties with Cuba. This is largely a decision based on broad strategic interests, as both countries seek to develop a presence in an area that the United States has traditionally sought to control—and in which the Obama administration had enjoyed considerable success. While there are commercial and investment possibilities that are of interest, far more important are the broader strategic opportunities presented by closer ties with Cuba. From Cuba's perspective, trade ties with China look more promising, while it is the political relationship with Russia that is most important.

Cuba-US Relations

The situation between Cuba and the United States has changed dramatically since 2014. While a major warming in US-Cuban relations took place under the Obama administration beginning in 2014, a diplomatic freeze quickly returned when Donald Trump assumed office in January 2017. Despite ominous signals from Washington, Cuba made it clear from the outset that it was prepared to work with the Trump administration, providing that it was treated with respect and as an equal partner in any negotiations without any preconditions. This approach was never reciprocated, and diplomatic tensions have steadily escalated since mid-2017.

Cubans talk sadly about the unfulfilled potential of "17/12"—December 17, 2014, when simultaneous TV broadcasts by Presidents Obama and Castro were made announcing that the two countries would restore diplomatic relations. Obama asserted: "In the most significant changes in our policy in more than fifty years, we will end an outdated approach that, for decades, has failed to advance our interests, and instead we will begin to normalize relations between our two countries."[33] Cubans had suffered a US embargo for over fifty years and were keen to see the economy opened up, foreign investment develop, and real wages increase. They agreed with Obama's clarity in his address: "Neither the American, nor Cuban people are well served by a rigid policy that is rooted in events that took place before most of us were born. . . . I do not believe we can keep doing the same thing for over five decades and expect a different result."

Under Obama, Cuban-US relations seemed headed in a direction that, apart from a short window during the Carter administration, had never before been seen. But there was an uneasy pace of change, with diplomatic advances rapidly overtaking any meaningful reform in commercial or trade matters. The embargo legislation from the early 1960s remained, and the relaxation in sanctions was wholly the result of presidential directives that a new executive could reverse—as Donald Trump has done in several instances. Cuba was still unable to export goods or merchandise to the United States, its natural market (with the exception of the license granted to test and potentially market CIMAvax, a lung cancer vaccine). At the same time, Havana seemed unsure about how much US trade and investment it wanted or could absorb, and the glacial pace in the bureaucratic framework was not conducive to encouraging American commercial commitments.

Despite the relative lack of success in commercial matters, bilateral relations improved significantly. In July 2015, full diplomatic relations were restored and embassies reopened in both capitals. Earlier in 2015, the Obama State Department removed Cuba from its list of countries allegedly supporting terrorism, and in 2014 the president commuted the sentences of three imprisoned Cuban intelligence agents. Cuba did the same for Alan Gross, a US Agency for International Development subcontractor, and allegedly a US intelligence asset. The two countries established bilateral working groups and a coordinating commission to engage in confidence-building measures that produced twenty-three bilateral key agreements by January 2017. Restrictions imposed by previous American administrations were relaxed, allowing far more US residents to visit Cuba. US investment on the island was now allowed in telecommunications and pharmaceuticals. An illustration of the potential of this new approach was the joint research and clinical trials of CIMAvax in Roswell Park, New York.

Among other innovations and reforms, US television programs were filmed in Havana, American cultural personalities visited, regular scheduled flights between several American cities and Cuba were established, and direct mail service between the two countries was renewed. In 2016, the Starwood Hotels chain became the first American company since 1959 to manage hotels on the island. Travel restrictions on American vessels were lifted, and dozens of cruise ships bringing tens of thousands of American visitors arrived. Havana was suddenly full of Americans, with a resulting boom among self-employed Cubans working in the hospitality industry. The Cuban government was allowed to open a bank account in the United States, and US companies as diverse as Airbnb and Netflix started to operate in Cuba. These initiatives represented an extraordinary reversal of several decades of hostility. William LeoGrande has summarized these advances well, noting how, in two years after the December 17 notification, "the two governments re-established diplomatic relations, expanded trade and travel, and signed 23 bilateral accords on issues of mutual interest. Some 60 US companies signed commercial deals with Havana, and the number of U.S. visitors jumped 57 percent between 2014 and 2016."[34]

Barack Obama carried this diplomatic initiative a step further when he visited Havana in March 2016 with his family and a delegation of members from the US Congress. It was the first visit of a sitting US president in eighty-eight years. In a nationally televised address in Cuba, he spoke about the advantages of free enterprise and praised Cuban entrepreneurs, criticized the Cuban record on human rights, and encouraged greater dialogue between both governments. He met with Cuban dissidents and civil society leaders, and together with Raúl Castro, attended a baseball game between a Cuban national team and Tampa Bay. Just prior to leaving office in January 2017, he ended the twenty-two-year-old "wet foot/dry foot" policy under which Cubans arriving on US territory had been automatically assumed to be eligible for "parole" status, which effectively gave them an unrestricted path to permanent residency. Since then, they have been processed in the same fashion as migrants from other nations. In addition, the US Department of Homeland Security ended the Cuban Medical Professional Parole Program, which had allowed Cuban doctors serving on humanitarian missions abroad to enter the United States legally if they defected. This policy, introduced by President George W. Bush, had been intended to cast doubt on Cuba's successful medical internationalism program in the Global South.

No variable is as important for the future of Cuban foreign policy as the relationship with the United States. At a time when Cuba is no longer ruled by a member of the Castro family, when there is a new president clearly interested in modernizing the economy and opening up to greater international connections, when the number of self-employed Cubans has multiplied almost 400 percent within a decade, and when there is a clear interest in developing—as with Obama—a normal foreign policy, a great deal depended on President Donald Trump's position regarding Cuba. The key question on this matter during the electoral process was: Would the Trump administration maintain the initiatives of his predecessor or revert to the previous Cold War strategy employed since 1960? The answer was not long in coming.

Elected in November 2016, the new US president made clear that he wanted to reverse the direction taken by his predecessor, even though he had sought to do business in Cuba and had spoken favorably of the improved relations prior to announcing his candidacy. Calling the agreements with

Cuba a "bad deal," Trump announced in a June 2017 Miami speech that his policy would now be aimed at regime change. In November the Treasury Department issued new travel regulations indicating that US citizens could take educational trips to Cuba only with a licensed provider, instead of on their own, and prohibiting American visitors from engaging with a list of over 180 hotels and businesses managed or owned by the Cuban military. (This list was also expanded on subsequent occasions.) In 2019 he followed this up by banning all American cruise ship traffic to Cuba, a policy that resulted in an estimated 500,000 American tourists being forced to change their Cuba travel plans. At the same time, the bilateral executive agreements on issues of mutual interest negotiated under President Obama remained in place, such as agreements on cooperation over environmental protection, natural disaster response, drug interdiction, law enforcement, and airline security.

A major deterioration in the bilateral relationship occurred in April 2019, on the anniversary of the 1961 Bay of Pigs invasion. The Trump administration announced that it would end the suspension of Title III of the 1996 Helms-Burton Act, which had been suspended by every American president until then. The act allows American citizens, including naturalized Cubans, to sue in American courts any companies in Cuba that benefit from any properties that had been confiscated by the Cuban government. Critics of this decision pointed out that for decades Washington had refused to allow affected Americans to negotiate compensation (unlike companies from many countries), and that the application of extraterritoriality went against international law. This process, potentially involving thousands of claims, could tie up American courts for many years. Not surprisingly, governments in several countries have condemned the move by the Trump administration.

Complicating matters were health problems that began to arise among US diplomats stationed in Cuba in late 2016. In August 2017, the Trump administration alleged that the incidents, which seem to have afflicted twenty-six Americans (an additional fourteen Canadian diplomats were affected as well), were due to "sonic attacks." Experts from the FBI and the RCMP flew to Havana to investigate the origins of these disturbing complaints but could find no explanation. Most of those complaining of the "sonic attacks" were examined by specialists at the University of Pennsylvania, but again there was no common medical explanation found. Cuba strongly denied any knowledge of the attacks and cooperated fully with requests from US and Canadian authorities. Nevertheless, the Trump administration blamed Cuba for the problem, arguing that it either was the perpetrator of "attacks," or at least knew who had undertaken them and had not stopped them. In response, the State Department reduced the US embassy staff by 60 percent and demanded that Cuba cut the size of its diplomatic mission in Washington by an equivalent number. With a total staff of only fifteen, the US embassy closed its consular section, which forced Cubans seeking legal entry to the United States to travel to Guyana or Colombia to apply for visas. As a result, fewer than five thousand Cubans were able to migrate to the United States in 2018, though the two countries had a legal agreement stipulating that at least twenty thousand Cubans would be granted visas for permanent residence annually. The consular problem also reduced the opportunities for Cubans to visit the United States for family visits, scientific and medical exchanges, educational purposes, and cultural events. In sum, bilateral ties were now severely limited.

The relation was further aggravated by the declaration in January 2019 by Juan Guaidó that he was the legitimate president of Venezuela. He claimed that the May 2018 presidential elections (in which Nicolás Maduro had been reelected) had been rigged and that therefore he—as president of the National Assembly—was the legitimate president. The Trump administration supported Guaidó and attacked the Maduro government, blocking access to Venezuelan government finances abroad, imposing pressure on the export of petroleum, aiding the political opposition, blacklisting the Maduro government, suspending flights from the United States to Venezuela, and even threatening military intervention. For its part, Cuba has remained firmly beside its ideological and commercial partner, and in turn has felt the wrath of Washington—which accuses the Cuban government (albeit with remarkably little evidence) of controlling both Maduro and the Venezuelan military. It is uncertain how this stalemate will end, although it is clear that pressure from the Trump administration will be maintained upon both Havana and Caracas—and that Cuba will continue its support for the Maduro government.

It is unlikely that future bilateral relations will improve before 2021 at the earliest. Indeed, given the US governance structure and the electoral college system, winning Florida in the November 2020 presidential election is crucially important for the incumbent. At a press conference on September 26, 2018, President Trump stated his position clearly: "I've been very proactive against Cuba. I don't like what's happening in Cuba. As you know, President Obama gave them a pass and I didn't like it. Neither do Cuban people based in Miami and based in our country that care for Cuba. I don't like what he did. I've ended much of it, most of it."[35] While he was exaggerating, there is no doubt that his administration did set back relations significantly.

Future Trends in Cuban Foreign Policy

Forecasting political trends is often both foolish and dangerous. In the case of Cuba there are many diverse elements at play that could affect the direction in which the government is headed. That said, there are some clear indications about the aspirations of the Díaz-Canel government. The basic goals of

Cuba's foreign policy are straightforward: encouraging greater initiative in pursuing foreign investment, diversifying trade relations, supporting the Global South in seeking appropriate processes of development, and developing alliances throughout the globe to defend itself against US attempts to bring about regime change. Under both Raúl Castro and Díaz-Canel, and specifically between 2014 and 2019, we saw the continuity of these policies—as well as some significant changes.[36] These are the same objectives assumed by President Díaz-Canel, and will undoubtedly continue. In his inaugural speech of April 2018, the incoming president made this abundantly clear: "Cuban foreign policy will remain unchanged and we reiterate that no one will be able to weaken the Revolution, nor make the Cuban people yield because Cuba does not make concessions against its sovereignty and independence. . . . We will never give in to pressure or threats."[37]

The greatest challenge facing Cuba at present is dealing with the policy of the United States under the current administration, the application of which has major economic and social implications. The distance between the two countries is just ninety miles, but the differences between the two governments reflect radically different worldviews and philosophies. Moreover, the existence of a group of senior advisors imbued with a Cold War ideology in the Trump administration does not bode well for the possibility of mutually beneficial relations, or even understanding. At the same time it is important to note that the Cuban government maintains solid diplomatic relations around the world. Often the image is projected in Western media that Cuba is isolated, when in fact that is definitely not the case. It has diplomatic relations with 195 states, and in 2018 some 33 heads of state, 9 vice presidents or deputy prime ministers, and 14 foreign ministers visited the island. The United Nations General Assembly vote condemning the US embargo in the fall of 2019 resulted in 187 countries supporting it, with only the United States, Brazil, and Israel voting against, and two abstentions. In sum, Havana has a normal diplomatic relationship with virtually every country in the world—with one glaring exception.

It is likely that Cuba's trading relations will continue to develop in ways that would have been inconceivable just five or six years ago. Venezuela, for example, comprised 44.2 percent of the island's trade in 2012 and was by far Cuba's most significant trading partner. By 2016, however, bilateral trade made up just 17.7 percent of Cuba's total international trade, behind China (20.5 percent).[38] With minor fluctuations, this trend will continue—resulting in the need for a greater diversification of trade and investment possibilities. China remains interested in increasing trade and investment with Cuba, but at the same time it insists on repayment of loans. Likewise, trade with Russia and investment with countries from the European Union seem certain to increase.

Cuba is a small country with a foreign policy akin to that of larger powers. It has defied the odds by surviving, despite decades of hostility from its powerful neighbor, just ninety miles away. It punches way above its weight in terms of humanitarian collaboration with the Global South, and it is widely respected globally. With a new president it is now developing an approach to foreign policy that is both based upon profoundly rooted political and philosophical values and in search of new initiatives. Much of the groundwork for this new approach was laid by the 2014–2018 period—an approach that has continued during the presidency of Díaz-Canel.

Events in November 2019 offered some valuable insights into the future. On November 1, and for the twenty-eighth time, the annual condemnation of the US embargo took place at the United Nations General Assembly. Clearly most countries and their leaders support Cuba's right to self-determination and would prefer a less belligerent approach from Washington. The same day as the UN condemnation of the embargo, however, John Bolton, the national security advisor of the Trump administration, condemned Cuba in an emotional speech in Miami, where he spoke of the "Troika of Tyranny" (Cuba, Venezuela, and Nicaragua) and vowed to increase pressure on Havana.

Also in early November 2018, newly elected Prime Minister Díaz-Canel arrived in Moscow, where he met with President Vladimir Putin, Prime Minister Dmitry Medvedev, and the leaders of both political chambers (Duma and the Council of the Russian Federation). This was the first step of a long diplomatic mission, first to France (where he was received by Prime Minister Edouard Philippe), and after the Russian leg of the journey to North Korea (meeting with Kim Jong Un), China (President Xi Jinping and Prime Minister Li Keqiang), Vietnam (President Nguyen Phu Trong), and Laos (President Bounnhang Vorachit), before a brief stop in London en route to Havana. Shuttle diplomacy has increased over the last two years, and government ministers and delegations have been actively seeking enhanced trade and investment possibilities, particularly throughout Europe and Asia.

The international relations scenario for Cuba was becoming obvious at this point. The government was clearly seeking to strengthen traditional political and commercial ties while seeking to develop new trading and investment opportunities. Troubled relations with Washington continued to play a major role in this strategy, an unfortunate development following the rapprochement established by Presidents Obama and Raúl Castro. On one side the Trump administration sought (largely without success) to condemn Cuba in international fora and to push for regime change, while on the other side Cuba's government was actively seeking to shore up support from traditional (and influential) allies who also expressed their displeasure with the Trump administration.

The future for Cuba looks complex, and the country's economy will face major challenges as increased US sanctions take effect, and as Venezuela's future hangs in the balance. Already increased food rations have been introduced, and there have been problems in the delivery of petroleum. The position of the Trump administration is starkly clear, as is seen in his April 30, 2019, threat to the Cuban government: "If Cuban Troops and Militia do not immediately CEASE military and other operations for the purpose of causing death and destruction to the Constitution of Venezuela, a full and complete embargo, together with highest-level sanctions, will be placed on the island of Cuba. Hopefully, all Cuban soldiers will promptly and peacefully return to their island."[39] A vivid contrast with this goal came the next day—the socialist holiday of May Day, when Raúl Castro was awarded the Order of Lenin, the highest civilian decoration bestowed by the Soviet Union. The following month saw the arrival in Havana harbor of a flotilla of Russian warships on a goodwill visit—the missile frigate *Admiral Gorshkov* and support vessels. With Chinese investment in the ascendancy, Russian political and military support increasing, and rhetoric from Washington adopting a menacing tone, it was beginning to look a lot like a reprise of the 1960s.

Chapter Four

Cuban Society

Becoming More Unequal, Connected, and Diverse

Katrin Hansing and Bert Hoffmann

Over the past six years, major political events have changed Cuban society, greatly affecting life at the grassroots level as well. We have witnessed the momentous decision by Presidents Barack Obama and Raúl Castro to normalize US-Cuban relations, revolutionary leader Fidel Castro's passing, the election of Donald Trump, and the handover of power from Raúl Castro to Miguel Díaz-Canel.

D-17, as the date of historic rapprochement between the United States and Cuba has come to be called, was met with tremendous excitement and joy by ordinary Cubans on the island. Church bells rang, cars honked, and strangers embraced each other on the streets after hearing the news. After more than fifty years of active, bilateral antagonism, which dominated and determined many aspects of Cubans' everyday lives, their family relations, and future prospects, the unimaginable happened. Overnight some of the heaviness and fatigue of the past five decades was lifted, and a palpable sense of hope and optimism filled the air. Many Cubans speculated that improved relations with the United States would bring greater economic opportunities and easier travel regulations between the two countries. Others hoped that the rapprochement with a longtime enemy might also be a sign that the Cuban government was itself opening up.

And indeed, between December 2014 and November 2016 it seemed like Cuba was changing and opening on many levels. Following the reestablishment of diplomatic relations between the United States and Cuba, commercial flights were reintroduced and US travel restrictions to Cuba were eased. This in turn led to a huge upsurge in American tourists, many of whom ironically wanted to see and experience "communist Cuba before it changes." Some of the more well-known visitors included President Obama and his family; the Rolling Stones, who gave a massive open-air concert in Havana; and designer Karl Lagerfeld, who hosted his annual Chanel fashion show along Havana's Prado. Businesspeople, members of Congress, heads of philanthropic organizations, Hollywood producers, and many more also flocked to the island to seek out potential opportunities.

In response to this wave of interested visitors and the general optimism about the future, hundreds of new, private businesses opened up on the island, energizing the private sector and real estate market as well as attracting private capital from abroad. For the first time in decades a real sense of energy and dynamism could be felt in the streets, and people's plans for the future began to be more about staying in Cuba than trying to figure out how to leave the island. Although it had taken twenty-five years longer than elsewhere, to many Cubans this period felt like their perestroika.

These winds of change, which seemed so unstoppable to most, began to gradually slow down after Obama's March 2016 visit to Cuba, which was strongly criticized by conservative forces within the Cuban government. The real blow, however, came with Donald Trump's unexpected election, followed a few weeks later by Fidel Castro's death. Fidel's passing literally brought the country to a standstill. Regardless of the many different, often strong, feelings and opinions Cubans have about Fidel Castro and his leadership, there is no doubt that he had a major influence on all Cubans' lives. The nine days of official national mourning seemed to be symbolic for what was yet to come.

With Trump's election it was clear that there would be some kind of rollback of Obama's Cuba policy. But the old, far-too-familiar political culture of antagonism returned more rapidly than expected. Mysterious health problems suffered by US embassy staff in Havana, followed by a de facto shutdown of the embassy and a temporary travel advisory for US citizens traveling to Cuba, caused US-Cuban relations to rapidly spiral downward and return to their former antagonistic self. In Cuba some people could not help but comment on the irony of the death of one autocrat and the rise of another, while others wished Fidel was still around to counter Trump's increasingly hostile rhetoric toward the island. As so often before, ordinary Cubans on both sides of the Florida Straits are the ones who have to bear the brunt of this political conflict.

As a result, American tourism to Cuba has declined, which in turn is adversely affecting the Cuban economy, including the private sector. Travel from Cuba to the United States has become very difficult, as Cubans now have to go to Guyana to apply for a US visa. And US business and philanthropic interest in Cuba has also dropped. At the same time, the Cuban government has put a brake on its own reforms (including pausing the issuance of certain licenses needed to open a private business) and begun to pressure, and in some cases even crack down on, members of civil society who are deemed too independent or critically minded. Within less than two years, US-Cuban rapprochement and Cuba's own domestic opening both took a 180-degree turn.

This has hit many Cubans hard. Many business and travel plans, as well as hopes and expectations, have been crushed, and once again uncertainty and cynicism have become widespread.

LOS LINEAMIENTOS: IMPACT ON THE LIVES OF ORDINARY CUBANS

Despite the importance of these recent events, Cuban society has arguably been mostly transformed of late by the economic and social reforms known as *Los Lineamientos de la Política Económica y Social* (*Lineamientos* for short). Introduced by Raúl Castro in 2011 with the aim of lifting Cuba out of its dire economic crisis, the reforms have included: large state worker lay-offs, serious cuts in social spending, the expansion of the private sector in the form of small businesses, comprehensive agricultural reform, a new tax code, and the legalization of the sale/purchase of private homes and cars between individuals. Moreover, the much criticized Cuban exit visa was eliminated in early 2013, giving Cubans the opportunity to travel more easily. As a result of these measures a new, mixed economy, made up of state, cooperative, and private sector enterprises, has emerged.

Although the reforms have been implemented slowly and in a stop-and-go manner, they have already had a huge impact on the lives of ordinary Cubans. After decades of rigid economic centralization, tight social controls, and travel restrictions, they are giving people more economic freedom as well as unprecedented mobility. During this time there has been an enormous growth in the number of new, private businesses as well as a huge increase in international travel by Cubans.[1] As a result, Cuban society has become more entrepreneurial, dynamic, independent, and transnational. However, the reforms have also produced unemployment and further outward migration, and they have increased already existing levels of poverty and socioeconomic inequalities.[2]

These negative trends are in part due to international factors such as the continued US embargo against Cuba and insufficient foreign direct investment, as well as a range of domestic, macro-economic challenges such as the lack of production on the island, low state wages, state employee layoffs, cuts in social spending, and increasing food and gas prices. The current pause in the economic reforms is also not helping to attract foreign investment, let alone build confidence in the Cuban economy.

Moreover, despite the increased liberalization of the private business sector, the Cuban state has so far failed to provide the population with the necessary credit system (i.e., loans, microcredits), infrastructure (wholesale markets), and resources (business training, etc.) to start or run a small business. This is particularly surprising given that the government's own reform logic expects a large number of the unemployed workers to join the private sector. As a result, it is mainly Cubans with access to private capital who can participate and take advantage of new economic opportunities such as starting a business, buying property or a car, and/or traveling. This situation is producing greater socioeconomic cleavages in Cuban society and causing much popular frustration.

SOCIAL INEQUALITIES

If the revolutionary, state-run economy and radical social policies of the 1960s were the main social elevators for the formerly underprivileged classes in socialist Cuba, the economic crisis and depressed wages of the past decades have seriously undercut these achievements. Poverty and social inequalities have been on the rise since 1990, the beginning of the Special Period, and the introduction of the dual currency system in 1993. Since then, Cuban society has become increasingly polarized between those who have access to Cuban Convertible Pesos (CUC) and those who do not, resulting in the formation of new socioeconomic stratifications. [3]

These stratifications tend to run along territorial (urban-rural; regional), gender, racial, and generational lines. Generally speaking, the southern and eastern parts of the island are economically less well developed than the northern and western provinces, and there are more economic opportunities in urban areas than rural ones. The most vulnerable groups include the elderly, single mothers, and Afro-Cubans. [4]

Cuba has a visibly growing number of wealthy people. They include owners of tourist-related private businesses, some private farmers, and successful artists, as well as some government officials. According to a survey in Havana, 20 percent of the population was poor (defined as "at risk of being unable to satisfy their basic needs") in 2000. Although statistics are unavailable, experts agree that the national figure is now considerably higher. Moreover, numbers are likely to grow if the government does not increase state wages, strengthen its social safety net, and create opportunities that benefit the unemployed and socioeconomically vulnerable so that they too can take advantage of the current economic reforms. Such opportunities might include access to microcredits, wholesale markets, business training, and affirmative action programs.

RACE AND INEQUALITY

The declining role of the state and introduction of market mechanisms has particularly affected Afro-Cubans. Inequality and racism, two key issues the revolution fought hard to eliminate, are thus once again thriving.

At the heart of Cuba's growing racial inequalities lies a complicated set of historical and contemporary factors, especially the Special Period. Since this time, all legal avenues to hard currency/CUC earnings (which are necessary for survival) have been highly correlated with race. For example, as Alejandro de la Fuente's work shows, Afro-Cubans have been discriminated against in the most lucrative economic sectors, such as tourism and joint ventures, because of racist hiring policies.[5] Also, due to their relative concentration in areas with run-down and overcrowded housing, the opening of private businesses such as bed-and-breakfasts or *paladares* has not been a viable option for most black families.

Furthermore, because the exile/émigré community is overwhelmingly white—85 percent of Cubans in the United States are phenotypically white[6]—most of the estimated US$3.5 billion in remittances they send to Cuba each year[7] benefits white households on the island.[8] Afro-Cubans only receive a small proportion of remittances and are thus clearly disadvantaged. This is also true for the large amount of material remittances, in the form of food, clothing, medicine, toiletries, home appliances, toys, and other commodities that are sent to families on the island. Moreover, with the increasing liberalization of the private sector there has been a strong reliance on private capital for starting up a new business or buying property. Most of this private capital is coming from the Cuban diaspora in the form of joint family investments or private loans and material resources.

Another important but less-known factor adding to the growing racial inequalities is foreign citizenship. In 2007, Spain passed the so-called Historic Memory Law, which offers Spanish citizenship to any person who can claim proof of a Spanish parent or grandparent. Due to strong Spanish immigration to Cuba in the 1920s and again under General Franco, the number of Cubans who can claim a Spanish grandparent is high; more than 140,000 Cubans have already obtained Spanish citizenship, and the Spanish consulate in Havana estimates that the total will go as high as 200,000. Most of these individuals are phenotypically white.

For Cubans, a Spanish—and hence EU—passport is the closest thing to winning the lottery, especially now that they no longer need an exit visa to leave Cuba. Not only does it allow for virtually worldwide, visa-free travel, but it also gives them the possibility of legally living and working almost anywhere in Europe. Although some Cubans are emigrating, most are using their new citizenship to temporarily work abroad or start a small business in Cuba. Taking advantage of the island's expanding private sector, continued material scarcities, and people's consumer desires, many are using their new passport to travel to nearby third countries (such as Mexico, Panama, the United States, and Haiti) and buy hard-to-get consumer goods, which they then resell with a handsome markup on the island.

Afro-Cubans are far less likely to have a cousin in Miami or a grandmother in Madrid who can send remittances, offer start-up capital for a small business, or provide a Spanish passport. With much less access to capital, goods, and mobility for Afro-Cubans, Cuba's new economic opportunities don't start from a level playing field and are clearly disadvantaging Afro-Cubans.

MANIFESTATIONS OF SOCIAL INEQUALITIES IN THE NEW CUBA

The effects of these growing socioeconomic divisions have started to become clearly visible and are manifesting themselves in different ways. Today most of the successful, private businesses in Cuba, whether *paladares*, bed-and-breakfast operations, beauty parlors, boutiques, or nightclubs, are not only owned but usually also managed, staffed, and frequented by white Cubans (as well as tourists) in urban or tourist areas along the northwestern coast of Cuba. Homes in exclusive neighborhoods continue to be bought and sold for exorbitantly high prices and restored to their former glory. A similar trend has also started in more run-down urban areas, where real estate is much cheaper, resulting in a process of gentrification.

The new economy has not only created new privileges but also enabled new lifestyles and habits. Some people have more money to spend on themselves and more time for leisure and recreation. It is thus not unusual to see imported cars on the streets of Havana or expensively dressed Cubans hanging out in many of the pricey restaurants and nightclubs. New high-end gyms, spas, and beauty parlors have cropped up, offering services such as yoga and Pilates, steam baths, and specialized nutritional diets.

Among economically well-off Cubans it is also common to have domestic help such as a housekeeper, nanny, gardener, and/or watchman. Unthinkable just a few years ago, it is also no longer unusual for Cubans with disposable income to spend their summer vacation in Europe or to go on a cruise. What would have been considered ostentatious and at times even counterrevolutionary behavior under Fidel Castro has become acceptable in the last decade.

These images of privilege stand in stark juxtaposition to the growing number of people who can be seen begging and rummaging through piles of garbage in search of food or recyclable cans and plastic bottles. Similarly, they contrast with the increasing numbers of devastatingly poor, urban shantytowns that are cropping up all around Havana as well as other provincial capitals along the northwest coast.

Most of the people who live in these slum-like dwellings, referred to in Cuba as "*llega y pon*," are Afro-Cuban migrants who have come from the island's even poorer eastern provinces.[9] They come in search of work in the parallel informal economies that have mainly sprung up where tourism is prevalent and/or where hard currency/CUC is in regular circulation. Most of these people live from day to day, making ends meet in whatever way they can. Because internal migration is not allowed in Cuba without permission from the state, these migrants are largely illegal, making their situation even more precarious. Due to their illegal status they cannot use their food ration card (*libreta*), with which all other Cubans receive a certain amount of basic subsidized food every month, because it is tied to a person's home address.

The urban tenement buildings (*solares*) and shantytowns that are mushrooming on the outskirts of cities and towns look like slums anywhere in the Global South, except that—and this is an important difference—children go to school, people have access to health care, and there is relatively little violent crime (especially when compared to neighboring countries in the region).

However, Cubans do not like comparing themselves to their neighbors in the region but rather to how things were before, especially before the Special Period. Moreover, they were brought up on a message of equality and social justice, and the social contract between the government and the people has been largely based on that expectation. There is no doubt that the Special Period changed many things and life became extremely difficult; but it was difficult for almost everyone. Now, with increasing social divisions, particularly the overt signs of wealth and privilege, this is changing, and people, especially among the have-nots, are increasingly frustrated. The fact that these social divisions can also be witnessed in the public sector, such as in health and education, is particularly exasperating.

SOCIAL SERVICES

Thirty years into the crisis that resulted from the Soviet Union's collapse, Cuba's celebrated health care and education systems have begun to show serious signs of deterioration. Although infant mortality is still low, maternal mortality has risen. Drugs, even aspirin and Band-Aids, are in short supply, and hospital patients have to bring their own sheets and food. Since 2013 there have been several serious outbreaks of cholera on the island, a disease that had not been seen in Cuba for over fifty years. Access to adequate and specialized care has also become increasingly difficult, given that almost forty thousand Cuban doctors and other health care workers are working in over sixty countries around the world. By sending its medical professionals abroad on "international medical missions," the Cuban government not only earns desperately needed hard currency but also keeps its high-quality health care reputation alive. This medical diplomacy is an important part of the island's foreign policy. Unfortunately, Cubans on the island are the ones who have to pay the price of not having adequate access to specialists at home.

Cuban health care and education have been a free and universal right for all Cubans since 1959. However, in practice, Cubans with financial, material, and social capital nowadays have better access to quality health care and education. In the public health sector this is happening because health care workers continue to earn low state wages and are thus easily inclined to accept a "gift" (*un regalito*) in the form of money and material goods or help a friend who will reciprocate the favor in some useful way. Bringing a *regalito* or having a friend in the health care sector allows for quicker and better medical attention. For instance, if one needs an appointment with a specialist, an X-ray, or an operation, a *regalito* will help secure and speed up the necessary care. People who don't have the means to offer a *regalito* or who don't have connections to someone in the health care system usually have to wait longer and often don't get the same quality care. This can have life-threatening consequences.

Similarly, in the education system, it has become standard for parents with means to hire private tutors (*repasador*) for their children after school. This practice became popular in the early 2000s when the quality of education drastically dropped due to the exodus of teachers from the public education sector, who left due to the low wages. To guarantee a moderate level of quality education and help their children get into university, parents started hiring private tutors, many of which, ironically, were the teachers who had left the public sector. Obviously, not all parents have the means to hire tutors for their children. In addition, many wealthy Cubans are sending their children abroad to study, a trend one can also observe among the ruling political class.

Over time a two-tier system has emerged within the public health and education sectors. For reasons already discussed, it is mainly the disadvantaged and vulnerable groups who don't have the means to offer a *regalito* or hire a *repasador*. One of the many effects of this situation is, for instance, that Afro-Cuban entry levels into the higher education system have significantly declined over the past years.[10]

Getting Connected: The Expanding Digital Landscape

Digital media have changed Cuba's urban landscape. At any time of day crowds of Cubans flock to the squares and parks, where the state monopoly telecom company ETECSA has installed Wi-Fi zones. This process began in

2014 and by the end of 2018 had reached a total of 830 in all major cities and towns across the island. More important than bringing new life to urban public spaces, the Wi-Fi zones have been a great leap in connecting Cubans to the world of digital media. This, in turn, has accelerated the dynamics of communication on the island and with family and friends abroad.[11]

Cuba has been a latecomer to the internet, not least due to the government's fear of losing control over media and communication.[12] While access in the public Wi-Fi zones remains rather slow, ETECSA introduced mobile 3G internet access on the island in December 2018. Costs are still high and the speed and coverage are not as fast and wide as Cubans would like. Nevertheless, this measure was a milestone in the long process of making digital media access part of everyday life on the island. In July 2019, ETECSA made broadband available in homes and businesses.[13]

Prices have gone down significantly from CUC$4.50 per hour in 2015 to CUC$1.00 per hour in 2018. As this remains costly for most Cubans, given the average monthly state salary of CUC$30, it has become a popular form of "remittances in kind"—that is, for emigrated Cubans to support their family on the island by recharging their cell phone and/or internet access accounts. More than 40 percent of the island's 11.2 million residents have a mobile phone contract. The actual hardware largely comes in through informal petty trade or with Cuban Americans, who bring along used phones, rather than by being bought as factory-new products in Cuba's state-run retail stores.

Cubans are incredibly inventive. As internet access has been and continues to be difficult and costly for many, much of the media content usually consumed via the internet is distributed in a sui generis work-around. The so-called *paquete semanal* (weekly package) has been described as an "offline Internet" and as "informal audio-visual consumption."[14] For a weekly fee of CUC$1.00, subscribers receive a regularly updated hard disk with as much as one terabyte of content, including everything from international and domestic news and entertainment, pirated software, local apps, and *Revolico*, the popular Cuban version of Craigslist.[15] With its vast offering of the latest Netflix movies and series, K-pop romances, homegrown music videos, and international sports events, *el paquete* is rapidly displacing Cuban television programming as the prime source of visual entertainment, especially among young and urban Cubans.

The production of *el paquete* has become an enormous industry, involving thousands of Cubans at various stages of its production. Time and again, political leaders bash it for not holding up high cultural values, but in practice *el paquete* is tolerated. The state-produced alternative, called *mi mochila* (the backpack) has failed to win a significant audience. The state does, however, monitor the content of *el paquete* and is very effective in ensuring self-censorship on the part of its producers. They know that any anti-government or pornographic material is off-limits and that the security apparatus would rapidly intervene and take them out of business if they did otherwise.

New Media, New Voices

Following in the footsteps of the early pioneers of the Cuban "blogo-sphere"[16] and with the spread of digital media, a wealth of new applications and media have sprung up in recent years.

In particular, a new form of grassroots journalism and a variety of media projects have emerged.[17] Some of these have grown out of earlier blogs, while others are completely new products. Although independent from the state, the majority are not defined by opposition to the government but rather are committed to a new, more dynamic, less top-down type of journalism. For instance, *Periodismo de Barrio*, founded by Elaine Díaz, carries well-written and researched articles on issues such as poor, neglected neighbor-hoods; communities affected by hurricanes, floods, or ecological problems not addressed by official media; and internal migration. *Vistar* nourishes the talk of the town with news, images, and gossip on the stars from Cuba's cultural and social scenes. "Play-off" is dedicated to sports; *El Toque* features fresh and critical storytelling that is not seen in the state or party press; and *Postdata* is Cuba's pioneer in developing a specific type of data-based journalism. And there are many more.

Given that Article 55 of the 2019 constitution asserts that "the State establishes the principles of organization and operation for all means of social communication," these new journalistic products move in a legal gray zone. The more politically outspoken they are, the thinner the ice on which they tread. *Cuba Posible*, for instance, had its roots in a magazine that was formerly published under the umbrella of the Catholic Church but over time evolved into an independent platform on political, social, and economic af-fairs—somewhere in between a magazine and an online think tank. While its promoters tended to see the project as an effort of "loyal opposition," the government repeatedly attacked it as an instrument of counterrevolution.[18] It ceased operation in May 2019.

The websites of a few openly dissident media platforms are blocked on the island, such as Yoani Sánchez's daily *14ymedio* or the video producer Estado de Sats. But most others are tolerated, although they are often re-minded of their precarious legal standing and the invisible limits of the permissible. Before becoming president, Miguel Díaz-Canel gave a speech at the Cuban Communist Party Academy in which he threatened a heavy hand against several independent media sites critical of the government.[19] The video was leaked and went viral on and off the island. Since then, journalists have been pressured not to cooperate with these media, while some other independent media have been added to the list of blocked websites. Although most of the emergent media continue their work, they often do so under difficult economic conditions and with weak institutional support.

Aside from these new media there are some platforms that have grown out of previously existing print publications, such as *Progreso Semanal* and *OnCuba*. In addition, a number of established cultural and social entities have expanded their media presence in the digital sphere. For instance, the well-known journal *Temas* now exists well beyond its quarterly print and online publication and includes an active blog (*Catalejo*) and regularly produces videos and DVDs from its monthly live panel discussion events (*Último Jueves*). In sum, over the past five years the Cuban media landscape has grown in size and scope and become much more diverse.

Social media have also become highly popular in Cuba. Any individual connected to the internet can become as much a recipient as a sender of data. And as the "Robertico incident" in September 2013 showed, people can have a real impact on political decisions. After what was considered a politically provocative performance by the popular singer Robertico Carcassés, state authorities banned him and his band from future performances. Carcassés made this sanction public on his Facebook page and posted a well-worded defense of his performance. He received so much solidarity and there were so many protests against the sanction that the government revoked it after a few days.[20]

Similarly, when the government announced a new law, decreto 349, that would effectively have tightened state control on cultural activities, the protests of many Cuban artists found effective voice in various digital and social media channels. The government insisted on having the controversial law come into effect on December 1, 2018, but immediately announced regulations that in practice suspended some of its most-criticized aspects.[21]

CONCLUSION

Contemporary Cuban society is arguably in an even more complicated and challenging place than it was after the collapse of the Soviet Union nearly three decades ago. For these and many other reasons its future remains uncertain. Much depends on the new leadership's willingness to continue to reform both the economy and the political system, without further compromising the Revolution's social gains. It also depends on US-Cuban relations and Cuba's continued integration into the regional and global communities. What is certain is that Cuba's reality, whether political, economic, social, or cultural, is not black and white but highly nuanced and constantly changing. And within this context Cubans, from all walks of life, will no doubt keep on being ingeniously creative in finding solutions to their many challenges.

Chronology of Key Events, 2014–2019

2014

January 28–29: The Second Summit of the Community of Latin American and Caribbean States (CELAC) takes place in Havana with President Raúl Castro chairing the conclave as the organization's co-president. CELAC's members include every state in the Western Hemisphere except the United States and Canada.

March 29: Cuba's National Assembly approves a new foreign investment law as part of the economic reforms to attract hard currency to the country.

May: The Council of Ministers approves the general bases for writing a 2016–2030 Social and Economic Development Program.

October: Cuba sends a medical brigade of 165 people—the largest foreign medical team from a single country—to Sierra Leone to fight the Ebola epidemic.

December 17: Presidents Raúl Castro and Barack Obama announce that their two countries will reestablish diplomatic relations. At the same time, Cuba releases Alan P. Gross on humanitarian grounds. Gross had been a USAID subcontractor charged with committing "acts against the integrity or territorial independence of the state" for installing sophisticated satellite communications transmitters, which may have included the capability of being undetectable for a radius of 250 miles. Gross and the US State Department claimed that his goal was to provide Cuba's Jewish community with equipment that would enable its members to access the internet without Cuban government interference. The United States releases the three remaining members of the Cuban Five still in US prisons in exchange for Cuba's release of a jailed US spy. The Five were Cuban intelligence officers who received long prison terms in 2001 after being convicted of conspiracy to commit espionage and murder. The Cuban government asserted that their mission was to monitor exile groups that had engaged in acts of terrorism against Cuba.

2015

January: The Cuban government commutes the sentences of fifty-three people whom the United States had identified as political prisoners.

April 9–11: Cuba participates for the first time in the Summit of the Americas, which is held in Panama. Castro and Obama engage in the first private bilateral meeting between a Cuban and US president.

May: The US State Department removes Cuba from its list of state sponsors of terrorism.

July 20: The Cuban and US embassies officially reopen in Washington, DC, and Havana, respectively.

July: The Cuban government begins the expansion of broadband Wi-Fi access throughout the country by creating "hotspots" at which users can connect to the Internet.

September 11: Cuba and the United States hold the inaugural session of a bilateral commission created to organize and provide continuity to the process of normalizing relations.

September 20–22: Pope Francis visits Cuba, during which time he officiates at three public masses.

September 29: Presidents Castro and Obama hold another bilateral meeting at the United Nations General Assembly.

2016

March 20–22: Obama visits Cuba along with his family and a bipartisan congressional delegation. Castro and Obama hold official meetings, give a joint press conference, and attend a baseball game between the Tampa Bay Rays and the Cuban National team. Obama gives a televised speech to the Cuban people from Cuba's National Theater, the Gran Teatro de La Habana Alicia Alonso.

March 25: The Rolling Stones perform at a free outdoor concert in Havana.

April 16–19: At the Cuban Communist Party's Seventh Congress, delegates approve resolutions affirming Cuba's socialist economic model and the proposed vision for the 2030 National Economic Development Plan, and they elect Raúl Castro as first secretary for a five-year term.

July 4–8: Castro reports to the National Assembly that Cuba's gross domestic product grew by only one percent in the previous year, half of what was planned.

August 24: The Colombian government and the Revolutionary Armed Force of Colombia (a guerrilla group engaged in armed struggle against the government since the 1960s) sign a peace agreement in Cuba. After Colombian voters reject the accord in a referendum, the parties renegotiate its terms in Havana. The Colombian Congress approves the final agreement on November 30.

October 14: Obama issues a Presidential Policy Directive (PPD-43), which consolidates changed policy with regard to Cuba, and the Treasury Department issues new regulations authorizing transactions related to Cuban-origin products, the sale of Cuban pharmaceuticals, joint medical research, and civil aviation safety-related services. This is the fifth package of regulatory reforms easing the embargo on Cuba issued by the Obama administration since December 17, 2014.

October 26: For the first time since 1992, when the UN General Assembly began annual votes on a resolution to end the US embargo, the United States and Israel abstain instead of voting against the resolution. The final vote is 191–0–2 in favor.

November 25: Fidel Castro Ruz dies at the age of ninety in Havana. Cuba declares nine days of mourning, a period that culminates in his burial on December 4 at Santa Ifigenia Cemetery in Santiago de Cuba.

December 12: Cuba and the European Union (EU) sign a Political Dialogue and Cooperation Agreement, which provides a framework for a relationship based on equality, reciprocity, and mutual respect. The signing comes in the wake of the EU's revocation of its 1996 Common Position conditioning economic cooperation on Cuba's human rights performance.

December: Cuban bilateral trade with China totals $1.8 billion in 2016, making China the island's second-largest trading partner.

2017

January 12: US officials meet in Havana for the third technical exchange on certified property claims by US nationals.

January 12: President Obama ends the 1995 policy known as "wet foot/dry foot" via executive order. Cubans arriving on US soil can no longer have an unrestricted path to permanent residency and are instead processed in the same fashion as migrants from other nations. The US Department of Homeland Security also ends the Cuban Medical Professional Parole Program, which allowed Cuban doctors serving on humanitarian missions abroad to enter the United States legally if they defected.

January 17: Cuba and the United States sign agreements to cooperate on air and maritime search and rescue in the Florida Straits.

January 31: The results of Cuba's 2016 national audit reveal business losses in Havana totaled over $50 million, reflecting a lack of oversight that accompanied decentralization.

February 3: The Trump administration announces it has begun a "thorough review" of policy toward Cuba.

February 16: President of Ireland Michael D. Higgens visits Cuba, the first time an Irish president has done so.

March 1: Panama and Cuba sign a memorandum of understanding on migration, concluding a series of talks between the two nations in Havana.

March 8: The Association of Caribbean States holds its first Cooperation Conference in Havana. The parties discussed new opportunities for cooperation, especially in development efforts.

March 30: Cuba releases a National Action Plan to prevent human trafficking.

April 10: Cuba invites UN special rapporteur Maria Grazia Giammarinaro to the island, the first time in a decade that a UN human rights special rapporteur has been allowed to visit Cuba.

May 3: Cuba and Russia sign an agreement allowing Cuba to purchase 1.9 million barrels of oil and diesel fuel from Russia, which eases pressure felt by the decline in Venezuelan imports.

May 22: Cuba opens five new *merca hostales* (wholesale markets) selling food items to *cuentapropistas*, bringing the total to eight *merca hostales*.

May 23: Two Cuban diplomats are expelled from the US embassy in Havana following an FBI investigation into what it alleges was exposure to a "covert device" that left several US diplomats with hearing loss.

June 16: Speaking in Miami at a theater named for the leader of the Cuban exile brigade that was defeated at the Bay of Pigs, President Trump announces that he is "canceling" President Obama's policy of engagement with Cuba and returning to a policy of hostility and regime change. On stage, he signs a National Security Presidential Memorandum imposing new trade and travel restrictions related to Cuba. The restrictions reverse an Obama policy that allowed Americans to undertake educational travel to Cuba without using a licensed tour provider, and they impose sanctions for engaging in commerce with entities controlled or operated by the Cuban military. The memorandum also creates a Cuba Internet Taskforce to examine "the opportunities for expanding Internet access and freedom of expression in Cuba."

June 23: Since the beginning of 2017, Cuban authorities have confiscated 1.8 tons of drugs, triple the amount taken in the same period in 2016. Cuba and the United States signed a Counter Narcotics Agreement one year ago that made increased cooperation and information sharing possible to prevent the illegal trafficking of narcotics.

July 5: The European Union Members of Parliament (MEPs) approve a Political Dialogue and Cooperation Agreement with Cuba by a vote of 567 to 65, with 31 abstentions. The accord dissolves the previous EU Common Position toward Cuba that had imposed sanctions on the island and includes "opposition to measures with extraterritorial effects" such as the US embargo.

July 13: Reports from state-run oil companies show that Cuba's oil imports from Venezuela slid almost 13 percent in the first half of 2017. Since 2016, Cuba has reduced fuel allocations by 28 percent to the majority of public companies.

September 9: Hurricane Irma reaches Cuba as a Category 5 storm, leaving ten dead and severely impacting the economy. The storm damages 300,000 hectares of sugarcane crops and 40 percent of Cuba's sugar refineries. The cost totals $13 billion, including over 150,000 homes damaged.

September 18: US and Cuban officials meet in Washington for the sixth session of the bilateral commission, the first to occur since the Trump administration took office.

September 29: The US State Department recalls 60 percent of its staff at the US embassy in Havana following allegations of "sonic attacks" on officials there; it also issues a travel advisory warning US residents against traveling to Cuba. In addition, the United States demands that Cuba reduce its embassy staff in Washington and designates the entire commercial section of the embassy withdrawn. Earlier in the week, Cuba reiterated its desire to cooperate with the United States in resolving these incidents at a speech to the UN General Assembly.

November 1: The United Nations approves a resolution condemning the US embargo against Cuba. Israel and the United States are alone in opposing the resolution, which passes with a vote of 191–2.

November 1: The Cuban-EU Political Dialogue and Cooperation Agreement goes into effect.

November 26: Armando Hart Dávalos dies at age eighty-seven. A founding member of the 26th of July Movement, he served as director of Cuba's 1961 literacy campaign, as minister of education, and as the first minister of culture.

December: Cuba ends the year with a record 4.7 million international visitors, including 620,000 from the United States. But the number of US travelers declined in December from the previous year as US State Department travel warnings began to have a negative impact.

December 21: Raúl Castro announces he will step down from the presidency in April 2018, rather than in February as previously planned, due to delays caused by Hurricane Irma.

2018

January 1: Policy changes announced in October via Cuba's *Gaceta Oficial* take effect. The estimated 800,000 Cubans living abroad no longer need an *habilitación* stamp on their passports in order to travel to the island. Children born abroad to Cuban citizens may also apply for citizenship.

January 3: Federica Mogherini, the EU's top diplomat, visits Havana to follow up with the implementation of the Political Dialogue and Cooperation Agreement, ratified in November 2017. Shortly after the visit, Cuba announces that the EU will invest $22.4 million over the subsequent five years in renewable energy projects on the island.

January 10: Cuba announces its intention to import an additional 2.1 million barrels of crude oil from Algeria in an attempt to make up for the loss of imports from Venezuela.

February 9: In an attempt to reverse its sagging birth rate and defuse a demographic time bomb, Cuba approves a decree giving parental leave to the grandparents of newborns.

February 14: A University of Pennsylvania examination of people affected by the health incidents at the US embassy in Havana finds evidence of "concussion-like" symptoms but cannot determine the cause.

February 26: Cigar manufacturer Havanos S.A. reports that Cuba's cigar sales reached a record $500 million in 2017, due largely to rapidly rising demand from China.

March 2: The US Department of State announces that the US embassy in Cuba will continue to operate with minimal personnel and orders making permanent the staffing changes it alleges resulted from "sonic attacks."

March: 83 percent of the electorate turns out to elect 605 deputies to the National Assembly and 1,265 delegates to Cuba's provincial assemblies. The process ends on April 19 when the National Assembly elects Miguel Díaz-Canel Bermúdez and Salvador Antonio Valdés

Mesa as the new president and first vice president, respectively, and the other twenty-nine members of the Council of State.

March 2: The OPEC Fund for International Development agrees to a $45 million loan for Cuba's Solar Energy Development Project, which aims to optimize the country's electric capacity through solar systems for businesses and homes. Cuba has a goal of generating 24 percent of the island's energy from renewable resources by 2030.

March 29: The US State Department announces that processing and interviews for immigrant visas for Cuban nationals are to be conducted in Georgetown, Guyana, rather than in Colombia, as they had been since January. In contrast to Colombia, Cubans do not need a visa to travel to Guyana; however, prices for flights are roughly double those for travel to Colombia. As part of the visa fallout, Cuba's National Symphony Orchestra cancels a 2019 trip to Chicago.

April 16: The United States and Cuba reestablish aerial postal service.

May 8–20: The Kennedy Center in Washington, DC, hosts the Festival of Cuban Arts, the largest-ever exhibition and celebration of Cuban art and culture in the United States, with more than one hundred Cuban artists, singers, dancers, and musicians participating.

May 29: Díaz-Canel denounces administrative corruption during a meeting discussing Cuba's 2019 Economic Plan and State Budget, calling it the "number one enemy of the Revolution."

May 30: Díaz-Canel travels to Venezuela to discuss strengthening the ties between the two nations with President Nicolás Maduro.

June 2: The Cuban National Assembly chooses Raúl Castro to lead the commission tasked with rewriting the Cuban constitution.

June 6: President Trump appoints former Miami mayor Tomás Regalado to head Radio and TV Martí, a US-based propaganda network. Regalado is a self-described "hard-liner" regarding Cuba policy.

July 10: The Cuban government announces private sector reforms that include requirements for labor contracts, sanctions for workplace discrimination, and limits on the number of licenses individuals and households can hold. All transactions will have to be carried out through state-run banks.

July 16: Cuba's state-run communications company begins providing data-based internet access to select mobile phones.

July 19: Under new socialist leadership, the Spanish government announces changes in its previous hard-line policy in order to open up dialogue with Cuba.

July 22: The Cuban National Assembly approves the first draft of the nation's updated constitution. It recognizes the right to own private property, promotes foreign investment, creates a new government position—prime minister—that will share duties with the president, abolishes provincial assemblies, and guarantees the right of same-sex persons to marry. At the same time, it reaffirms the socialist nature of Cuban society and the leading role of the Communist Party.

September 4: As part of its ongoing effort to support the peace process in Colombia, Cuba receives the first of two hundred scholarship recipients participating in a Cuban program to assist veterans of the Colombian civil war in finding new career paths.

September 26: During his first visit to the United States, Díaz-Canel addresses the UN General Assembly, denouncing recent US policies of unilateralism and sanctions, yet emphasizing the importance of maintaining a positive relationship between the two countries.

September 26: The first-ever biotech venture between the US and Cuba, named Innovative Immunotherapy Alliance S.A., is announced. The venture is intended to research new cancer treatments and promote new, potentially life-saving medications.

November 1: With a vote of 188–2–0, the United Nations General Assembly votes again for a resolution to end the US embargo of Cuba. Israel and the United States vote in opposition.

November 1: In a Miami speech the week before the midterm elections, US national security advisor John Bolton calls Cuba, Venezuela, and Nicaragua a "Troika of Tyranny" and announces there will be new sanctions against the three countries.

November 1: Díaz-Canel arrives in Moscow, marking the beginning of an international tour that takes him also to North Korea, China, Vietnam, Laos, and the United Kingdom.

November 14: Cuba announces it will withdraw most of the 8,600 doctors working in rural Brazilian towns under a Pan American Health Organization program in response to President-Elect Jair Bolsonaro's demand that the doctors obtain new licenses, and that they receive 100 percent of the salaries paid by the Brazilian government.

November 14: The Trump administration adds twenty-six popular tourist attractions in Cuba, including sixteen hotels, to the State Department's list of places Americans are prohibited from visiting.

December 6: The day before new restrictive regulations on the private sector go into effect, the government responds to complaints by private entrepreneurs by eliminating two of the most criticized provisions limiting licenses and the size of restaurants. The government also promises to consult with Cuban artists before implementing a new restrictive law on the arts.

December 6: Cubans gain internet access via cell phones as ETECSA, the state-owned telecommunications company, begins 3G service for everyone.

December 19: US Major League Baseball announces an agreement with the Cuban Baseball Federation intended to facilitate the hiring of Cuban baseball players by US professional teams.

December: The number of international visitors to Cuba increased slightly in 2018 to 4.75 million, but the number from the United States declined by 6.8 percent.

2019

January 5: Cuban government publishes the final draft of the new constitution. Its provisions on political rights, such as habeas corpus and guaranteeing arrested persons the right to legal representation, have greater detail and specificity than they did in the initial July 2018 draft. But the provision guaranteeing the right of same-sex persons to marry in the original was discarded.

January 7: Florida International University releases its 2018 poll of Cuban Americans. While respondents were evenly split between those favoring and opposing continuation of the US embargo against Cuba, 68 percent favored US companies expanding or maintaining business relation with the island.

January 28: Within hours of the worst tornado ever to hit Havana, Cubans use newly acquired cell phone Wi-Fi access to mobilize support for the victims via social media apps. The tornado killed four and injured 195.

February 6: Russia announces that it has approved a $43 million loan to Cuba for the purpose of purchasing military equipment such as armored vehicles.

February 24: Cuban voters approve the new constitution in a referendum, with 87 percent voting in favor. Turnout was 84.4 percent of the 8.7 million possible voters. Opponents of the constitution—mainly the Roman Catholic Church and evangelical Protestant churches—were permitted to campaign publicly against it, the first time the government has allowed such activity on a referendum.

April 8: President Trump cancels the agreement between Major League Baseball and the Cuban Baseball Federation that would have established a system for legally enabling Cuban players to join US professional teams.

April 17: Despite opposition from US allies, President Trump announces he will not waive Title III of the 1996 Cuban Liberty and Democratic Solidarity (Libertad) Act, also known as the Helms-Burton Act. Since its passage, Republican and Democratic presidents had waived Title III, which permits US citizens to sue in US court corporations and individuals "trafficking" in property of theirs expropriated by the Cuban government, even if the persons had not been US citizens at the time of the expropriation.

May 10: In the wake of widespread food shortages and a decline in hard currency earnings, the Ministry of Internal Commerce announces the government will ration the sale of chicken, eggs, rice, beans, and several hygienic products such as soap.

June 5: The US Treasury and Commerce Departments issue regulations canceling licenses for organizations engaged in "people-to-people" education travel for Americans, prohibiting US-based cruise ships from docking at Cuban ports, and capping at $1,000 every three months the previously unlimited remittances Americans could send to their families in Cuba.

Useful Websites

OFFICIAL CUBAN WEBSITES

Cuban president's office: http://www.presidencia.gob.cu/es

Raúl Castro's speeches: http://www.cuba.cu/sites/politica/discursos-del-presidente--raul-castro-ruz

Fidel Castro's speeches: http://www.cuba.cu/gobierno/discursos

Communist Party of Cuba: https://www.pcc.cu/es

Cuban Embassy in the United States: https://misiones.minrex.gob.cu/es/eeuu

Ministry of Foreign Relations: http://www.minrex.gob.cu

National Assembly: http://www.parlamentocubano.gob.cu

Oficina Nacional de Estadísticas, Cuba: http://www.one.cu

Cuban Center for National Sexual Education: https://www.facebook.com/cenesex

Academia de Ciencias de Cuba: http://www.academiaciencias.cu

CubaDebate: http://www.cubadebate.cu/categoria/noticias

US GOVERNMENT WEBSITES

US State Department—Cuba: https://www.state.gov/countries-areas/cuba

US Embassy Cuba: https://cu.usembassy.gov

CIA World Fact Book—Cuba: https://www.cia.gov/library/publications/the-world-factbook/geos/print_cu.html

USAID—Cuba: https://www.usaid.gov/cuba

US Treasury Department, Office of Foreign Assets Control—Cuba: https://www.treasury.gov/resource-center/sanctions/Programs/Pages/cuba.aspx

US Trade with Cuba data: https://www.census.gov/foreign-trade/balance/c2390.html

RESEARCH INSTITUTES AND ADVOCACY GROUPS

Center for Democracy in the Americas: http://democracyinamericas.org
National Security Archive, Cuba Project: https://nsarchive.gwu.edu/project/cuba-project
Washington Office on Latin America, Cuba Project: https://www.wola.org/program/cuba
Brookings Institution—Cuba: https://www.brookings.edu/topic/cuba
Center for Cuban Studies: http://centerforcubanstudies.org
Cuba Study Group: http://cubastudygroup.org
American University Center for Latin American and Latino Studies, Cuba Initiative: https://www.american.edu/centers/latin-american-latino-studies/cuba-initiative.cfm
Council on Foreign Relations—Cuba: https://www.cfr.org/backgrounder/us-cuba-relations
US-Cuba Business Council: https://www.uschamber.com/us-cuba-business-council
Engage Cuba: https://www.engagecuba.org
Association for the Study of the Cuban Economy: https://www.ascecuba.org
Cuban Commission for Human Rights and National Reconciliation: http://ccdhrn.org
Cuba Money Project: http://cubamoneyproject.com
Florida International University Cuba Poll: https://cri.fiu.edu/research/cuba-poll
Cuba Research Institute, FIU: https://cri.fiu.edu
New York Times—Cuba: https://www.nytimes.com/topic/destination/cuba
The Cuban Economy: https://thecubaneconomy.com
Cuba Educational Travel: https://www.cubaeducationaltravel.com
Havana Consulting Group: http://www.thehavanaconsultinggroup.com
Center for a Free Cuba: https://www.cubacenter.org
Human Rights Watch—Cuba: https://www.hrw.org/americas/cuba
Amnesty International—Cuba: https://www.amnesty.org/en/countries/americas/cuba
American Enterprise Institute—Cuba: http://www.aei.org/tag/cuba
Cuban American National Foundation: https://www.canf.org
History of Cuba: http://www.historyofcuba.com
Cuban baseball: http://www.baseballdecuba.com

MEDIA

Cuban Studies: http://muse.jhu.edu/journal/260
International Institute for the Study of Cuba and *International Journal of Cuban Studies*: http://cubastudies.org
Bohemia: http://bohemia.cu
La Jiribilla (Cuban culture magazine): http://lajiribilla.cu
El Nuevo Herald: https://www.elnuevoherald.com
Miami Herald: https://www.miamiherald.com
Inter Press Service in Cuba: https://www.ipscuba.net
Agencia Cubana de Noticias: http://www.acn.cu
Prensa Latina: https://www.prensa-latina.cu
Granma (English): http://en.granma.cu
Granma (Spanish): http://www.granma.cu
Juventud Rebelde: http://www.juventudrebelde.cu
El Toque: https://eltoque.com
Temas: http://www.temas.cult.cu
La Joven Cuba: https://jovencuba.com
Progreso Semanal: https://progresosemanal.us
14ymedio: https://www.14ymedio.com
Cuba Standard: https://www.cubastandard.com
Cuba Posible (ceased updating in May 2019): https://cubaposible.com
OnCuba: https://oncubanews.com
Vistar: https://vistarmagazine.com
Havana Times: https://havanatimes.org
Periodismo de Barrio: https://www.periodismodebarrio.org
La Pupila Insomne: https://lapupilainsomne.wordpress.com
Translating Cuba: https://translatingcuba.com
Café Fuerte: http://cafefuerte.com
Radio & TV Martí https://www.radiotelevisionmarti.com
Diario de Cuba: http://www.diariodecuba.com

BLOGS AND TWITTER

President Díaz-Canel's Twitter: https://twitter.com/DiazCanelB
Cuban Triangle: http://cubantriangle.blogspot.com
Along the Malecon: https://alongthemalecon.blogspot.com
Pedro Monreal: https://elestadocomotal.com
Elaine Diaz's *La Polémica Digital*: https://espaciodeelaine.wordpress.com
Silvio Rodriguez's *Segunda Cita*: https://segundacita.blogspot.com

Excerpts from Primary Documents

THE CONSTITUTION OF THE REPUBLIC OF CUBA, 2019

Preamble

WE, THE PEOPLE OF CUBA,

inspired by the heroism and patriotism of those that fought for a free, independent, sovereign, and democratic homeland of social justice and human solidarity, forged through the sacrifice of our ancestors;

by the indigenous peoples who resisted submission;

by the slaves that rebelled against their masters;

by those that awoke the national conscience and Cuban desire for our liberty and homeland;

by the patriots that started and participated in our struggles for independence against Spanish colonization beginning in 1868 as well as those whose final efforts of 1895 were denied victory with the beginning of the military intervention and occupation of Yankee imperialism in 1898;

by those that fought for over fifty years against imperialist domination, political corruption, the lack of rights and liberties, unemployment, the exploitation imposed by capitalists, landowners, and other social evils;

by those who promoted, participated in, and developed the first organizations of laborers, farm workers, and students; disseminated socialist ideas; and founded the first revolutionary, Marxist, and Leninist movements;

by the members of the vanguard of the generation of the 100th anniversary of Martí's birth, who, nourished by his teaching, led us to the victorious popular revolution in January of 1959;

by those that, in sacrificing their lives, defended the Revolution and contributed to its definitive consolidation;

by those that completed heroic international missions together;
by the epic resistance and unity of our people;

GUIDED

by the most advanced revolutionary, anti-imperialist, Cuban-Marxist, Latin American, and universal thought, in particular by the ideal and example of Martí and Fidel, as well as the social emancipation ideas of Marx, Engels, and Lenin;

SUPPORTED

in proletariat internationalism, fraternal friendship, the help, cooperation, and solidarity of the peoples of the world, particularly those of Latin America and the Caribbean;

DETERMINED

to carry forward the triumphant Revolutions of Moncada and Granma, of the Sierra, of the underground struggle, and of Girón that, sustained in the contribution and unity of the principal revolutionary forces and the people, conquered full national independence, established revolutionary power, realized the democratic transformations and initiated the construction of Socialism;

COMMITTED

to Cuba never returning to capitalism as a regime sustained by the exploitation of man by man, and that it is only in socialism and communism that a human being can achieve his or her full dignity;

CONSCIOUS

that national unity and the leadership of the Communist Party of Cuba, born through the unitary will of the organizations that decisively contributed to the triumph of the Revolution and legitimized by the people, constitute fundamental pillars and guarantees of our economic, social and political order;

IDENTIFIED

with the tenets displayed in the concept of Revolution, as expressed by the Commander in Chief Fidel Castro on the 1st of May of the year 2000;

WE DECLARE

our will that the law of the laws of the Republic be presided over by this profound yearning, finally achieved by José Martí, "I wish that the first law of our Republic be the devotion of the Cubans to the full dignity of man";

WE ADOPT

by our free and secret vote, through a popular referendum, one hundred and fifty years after our first Mambí Constitution, approved in Guáimaro on April 10, 1869, the following:

Title I: Political Foundations

ARTICLE 1. Cuba is a democratic, independent and sovereign socialist State of law and social justice, organized by all and for the good of all, as an indivisible and unitary republic, founded by the labor, dignity, humanism, and ethic of its citizens for the enjoyment of liberty, equity, justice, and equality, solidarity, and individual and collective well-being and prosperity.

. . .

ARTICLE 5. The Communist Party of Cuba, unique, Martiano, Fidelista, and Marxist-Leninist, the organized vanguard of the Cuban nation, sustained in its democratic character as well as its permanent linkage to the people, is the superior driving force of the society and the State.

It organizes and orients the communal forces towards the construction of socialism and its progress toward a communist society. It works to preserve and to fortify the patriotic unity of the Cuban people and to develop ethic, moral, and civic values.

. . .

ARTICLE 15. The State recognizes, respects, and guarantees religious liberty.

The Republic of Cuba is secular. In the Republic of Cuba, the religious institutions and fraternal associations are separate from the State and they all have the same rights and duties.

Distinct beliefs and religions enjoy equal consideration.

. . .

Title II: Economic Foundations

ARTICLE 18. The Republic of Cuba is governed by a socialist economic system based on ownership by all people of the fundamental means of production as the primary form of property as well as the planned direction of the economy, which considers, regulates, and monitors the economy according to the interests of the society.

. . .

ARTICLE 28. The State promotes and provides guarantees to foreign investment as an important element for the economic development of the country, which is based upon the protection and the rational use of the natural and human resources as well as respect for national sovereignty and independence.

The law establishes regulations with respect to foreign investment within the national territory.

. . .

ARTICLE 30. The concentration of property in natural or legal non-state persons is regulated by the State, which also guarantees an increasingly just redistribution of wealth in order to conserve the limits that are compatible with the socialist values of equity and social justice.

The law establishes regulations that guarantee its effective enforcement.

Title V: Rights, Duties, and Guarantees

Chapter I: General Provisions

. . .

ARTICLE 42. All people are equal before the law, receive the same protection and treatment from the authorities, and enjoy the same rights, liberties, and opportunities, without any discrimination for reasons of sex, gender, sexual orientation, gender identity, age, ethnic origin, skin color, religious belief, disability, national or territorial origin, or any other personal condition or circumstance that implies a distinction injurious to human dignity.

All people have the right to enjoy the same public spaces and service facilities.

Likewise, they receive equal salary for equal work, with no discrimination whatsoever.

The violation of this principle is proscribed and is sanctioned by law.

ARTICLE 43. Women and men have equal rights and responsibilities in the economic, political, cultural, occupational, social, and familial domains, as well as in any other domain. The State guarantees that both will be offered the same opportunities and possibilities.

The State encourages the holistic development of women and their full social participation. It ensures the exercise of their sexual and reproductive rights, protects them from gender-based violence in all of its forms and in all spaces, and creates the institutional and legal mechanisms to do so.

Chapter II: Rights

. . .

ARTICLE 58. All people have the right to enjoy their personal property. The State guarantees its use, enjoyment, and free disposal, in accordance with what is established in the law.

The expropriation of goods is solely authorized for the purpose of attending to reasons of public utility or social interest with the required indemnity.

The law establishes the means to determine their utility and necessity, the required guarantees, and the procedure for their expropriation and the form of indemnity.

. . .

ARTICLE 68. People who work have a right to social security. The State, through the social security system, guarantees adequate protection when a person finds themselves unable to work due to age, maternity, paternity, disability, or illness. . . .

ARTICLE 69. The State guarantees the right to safety and health at work through the adoption of suitable means to prevent work-related accidents or illnesses. . . .

ARTICLE 70. The State, through social assistance, protects persons without resources or shelter, those who are unable to work, those without family members who are able to care for them, and the families that, due to low income, require it, according to the law.

ARTICLE 71. The State recognizes the right to adequate housing and a safe and healthy home for all people. . . .

ARTICLE 72. Public health is a right of all people and it is the State's responsibility to guarantee access to quality medical attention, protection, and recovery services, free of charge.

The State, in order to effectuate this right, institutes a healthcare system at all levels that is accessible to the population and develops prevention and education programs, in which the society and families contribute. . . .

ARTICLE 73. Education is a right of all people and the responsibility of the State, which guarantees free, accessible, and quality education services to its citizens for their holistic development, from preschool until the postgraduate level.

. . .

Chapter VI: Guarantees of Rights

ARTICLE 96. Anyone illegally deprived of liberty, of their own account or by a third party, has the right to submit a writ of Habeas Corpus to a competent court, according to the requirements established in the law.

Sources: English translation: Constitute Project, https://www. constituteproject.org/constitution/Cuba_2019?lang=en; original Spanish: *Granma International*, http://www.granma.cu/file/pdf/gaceta/Nueva%20 Constituci%C3%B3n%20240%20KB-1.pdf.

TREASURY AND COMMERCE IMPLEMENT
CHANGES TO CUBA SANCTIONS

WASHINGTON—Today, the Department of the Treasury's Office of Foreign Assets Control (OFAC) unveiled amendments to the Cuban Assets Control Regulations (CACR) to further implement the President's foreign policy on Cuba. These amendments complement changes to the Department of Commerce's Bureau of Industry and Security (BIS) Export Administration Regulations (EAR), which Commerce is also unveiling today. These regulatory changes were announced on April 17, 2019 and include restrictions on non-family travel to Cuba.

"Cuba continues to play a destabilizing role in the Western Hemisphere, providing a communist foothold in the region and propping up U.S. adversaries in places like Venezuela and Nicaragua by fomenting instability, undermining the rule of law, and suppressing democratic processes," said Treasury Secretary Steven Mnuchin. . . . These actions mark a continued commitment towards implementing the National Security Presidential Memorandum signed by the President on June 16, 2017 titled "Strengthening the Policy of the United States Toward Cuba." These policies continue to work to channel economic activities away from the Cuban military, intelligence, and security services. . . .

Major elements of the changes in the revised regulations include:

Ending Group People-to-People Travel

• In accordance with the newly announced changes to non-family travel to Cuba, OFAC is amending the regulations to remove the authorization for group people-to-people educational travel. OFAC's regulatory changes include a "grandfathering" provision, which provides that certain group people-to-people educational travel that previously was authorized will continue to be authorized where the traveler had already completed at least one travel-related transaction (such as purchasing a flight or reserving accommodation) prior to June 5, 2019. . . .

Ending Exports of Passenger Vessels, Recreational Vessels, and Private Aircraft

• BIS, in coordination with OFAC, is amending the EAR to make passenger and recreational vessels and private and corporate aircraft ineligible for a license exception and to establish a general policy of denial for license applications involving those vessels and aircraft.

Source: Press Release, US Department of the Treasury, Office of Public Affairs, June 4, 2019, https://home.treasury.gov/news/press-releases/sm700.

CANADIAN GOVERNMENT POSITION ON
HELMS-BURTON TITLE III

May 3, 2019—Ottawa, Ontario—Global Affairs Canada and Department of Justice Canada

The Honourable Chrystia Freeland, Minister of Foreign Affairs, and the Honourable David Lametti, Minister of Justice and Attorney General of Canada, today issued the following statement regarding Canadian businesses operating in Cuba:

"As of May 2, 2019, the United States government has fully implemented Title III of the Cuban Liberty and Democratic Solidarity (LIBERTAD) Act of 1996, commonly known as the Helms-Burton Act.

"Canada's opposition to the Helms-Burton Act is based on the principles of international law and reflects our long-standing objection to the extraterritorial application of laws by another country.

"Canada has had measures in place since 1996 under its Foreign Extraterritorial Measures Act (FEMA) to help protect Canadians and Canadian businesses and the workers they employ. Our FEMA legislation is strong and we are prepared to apply it.

"As stated in FEMA, no judgment issued under Title III of the Helms-Burton Act will be recognized or enforced in any manner in Canada. FEMA also allows Canadians to use Canadian courts to sue the person who has initiated an action under Helms-Burton, even while proceedings are still ongoing. This will allow Canadians to recover any amounts that have been obtained against them, including legal expenses, and losses or damages incurred.

"The Government of Canada will always defend Canadians and Canadian businesses conducting legal trade and investment with Cuba, and is reviewing all options in response to the US decision. Canada will also continue to work with our international partners, including the EU, to stand up for our businesses."

Source: "Statement from Government of Canada for Canadians Doing Business in Cuba," May 3, 2019, https://www.canada.ca/en/global-affairs/news/2019/05/statement-from-government-of-canada-for-canadians-doing-business-in-cuba.html.

CUBAN GOVERNMENT RESPONSE TO
IMPLEMENTATION OF HELMS-BURTON ACT TITLE III

Declaration of the Revolutionary Government of Cuba

Today, the 17th of April, we celebrate another anniversary of the start of the military aggression at the Bay of Pigs (Playa Girón) in 1961. The decisive response of the Cuban people in defense of the Revolution and socialism resulted in the first military defeat of imperialism in the Americas, in just 72 hours.

Oddly enough, it is the date chosen by the current government of the United States to announce the adoption of new aggressive measures against Cuba and to reinforce the application of the Monroe Doctrine.

The Revolutionary Government rejects in the most energetic of terms the decision to permit hereinafter that action is taken in US courts against Cuban and foreign entities outside the jurisdiction of the United States, and that of intensifying the impediments for entry into the United States of the executives of companies that legally invest in Cuba and their relatives in properties that were nationalized. These are actions envisaged in the Helms-Burton Act that were rejected a long time ago by the international community, that the Cuban nation has repudiated from the time when they were enacted and applied in 1996, and whose fundamental aim is to impose colonial protection over our country.

Cuba also repudiates the decision to return to limiting the remittances which Cuban residents in the US send to their families and next of kin, to restrict even further travel by American citizens to Cuba and to apply additional financial penalties.

It energetically rejects the references that in Cuba attacks have been produced against American diplomats. They would like to justify their actions, as usual, using lies and blackmail. On last 10 April, General of the Army Raúl Castro declared: "Cuba is blamed for all evils, using lies in the worst style of Hitlerian propaganda."

To cover up and justify the evident failure of the sinister coup d'état manoeuver of designating, from Washington, a usurper "president" for Venezuela, the government of the United States resorts to slander. It accuses Cuba of being responsible for the soundness and steadfastness shown by the Bolivarian and Chavista government, the people of that country and the civilian-military union which defends the sovereignty of their nation. It brazenly lies when it declares that Cuba keeps thousands of troops and security forces in Venezuela, influencing and determining what is happening in that sister country.

It has the cynicism of blaming Cuba for the economic and social situation besetting Venezuela after years of brutal economic penalties, conceived and

applied by the United States and a number of allies, precisely to economically suffocate the population and to cause its suffering. Washington has gone to
the extremes of pressuring the governments of third countries to attempt to
persuade Cuba to withdraw this presumed and unlikely military and security
support and even for it to stop providing backing and solidarity to Venezuela. . . .

It must remain absolutely clear that steadfast solidarity with the sister
Bolivarian Republic of Venezuela is Cuba's right as a sovereign State and it
is also a right that forms part of the tradition and essential principles of the
foreign policy of the Cuban Revolution. No threats of reprisals against Cuba,
no ultimatum or blackmail by the current US government is going to divert
the internationalist conduct of the Cuban nation, despite the devastating human and economic damages caused our people by the genocidal blockade. . . .

The Government of Cuba calls on all members of the international community and on the citizens of the United States to stop the irrational escala-
tion and the policy of hostility and aggression of the government of Donald
Trump. With complete justification, year after year the Member States of the
United Nations have called practically unanimously for the end to this economic war. The peoples and governments of our region must see to it that,
for the benefit of all, the principles of the Proclamation of Latin America and
the Caribbean as a Zone of Peace prevail.

Last April 13th, the President of the Councils of State and Ministers
Miguel Díaz-Canel Bermúdez declared: "Cuba continues to trust in its
strength, its dignity and also in the strength and dignity of other independent
and sovereign nations. But it also continues to believe in the American people, in the Land of Lincoln, that they should be ashamed of those who act on
the fringes of universal law on behalf of the entire American nation". . . .

[T]he Cuban Revolution reiterates its firm determination to face up to and
prevail over the escalated aggression of the United States.

Havana, 17 April 2019

Source: Ministry of Foreign Relations of Cuba, April 19, 2019, http://
misiones.minrex.gob.cu/en/articulo/declaration-revolutionary-government-
cuba-2.

SECRETARY OF STATE MIKE POMPEO ON ENDING WAIVER OF THE HELMS-BURTON ACT TITLE III (APRIL 17, 2019)

In 1996, Congress passed the Cuban Liberty and Democratic Solidarity Act, also known as the Libertad Act. Until Title III of that act, United States citizens who had their property confiscated by the Castro regime were given the right to file suit against those who traffic in such properties.

But those citizens' opportunities for justice had been put out of reach for more than two decades. For now more than 22 years, every president, every secretary of state has suspended Title III in the hope that doing so would put more pressure on the Cuban regime to transition to democracy. . . .

We see clearly that the regime's repression of its own people and its unrepentant exportation of tyranny in the region has only gotten worse because dictators perceive appeasement as weakness, not strength.

President Obama's administration's game of footsy with the Castros' junta did not deter the regime from continuing to harass and oppress the heroic Ladies in White, a group of women dedicated to peacefully protesting the regime's human rights abuses.

More broadly, the regime continues to deprive its own people of the fundamental freedoms of speech, press, assembly, and association. . . .

Cuba's behavior in the Western Hemisphere undermines the security and stability of countries throughout the region, which directly threatens United States national security interests. The Cuban regime has for years exported its tactics of intimidation, repression, and violence. They've exported this to Venezuela in direct support of the former Maduro regime. Cuban military intelligence and state security services today keep Maduro in power.

Sadly, Cuba's most prominent export these days is not cigars or rum; it's oppression. Détente with the regime has failed. Cozying up to Cuban dictators will always be a black mark on this great nation's long record of defending human rights.

For these reasons, I'm announcing that the Trump administration will no longer suspend Title III. Effective May 2nd, the right thing to bring—the right thing to bring an action under Title III of the Libertad Act will be implemented in full. . . .

Implementing Title III in full means a chance at justice for Cuban Americans who have long sought relief for Fidel Castro and his lackeys seizing property without compensation. For the first time, claimants will be able to bring lawsuits against persons trafficking in property that was confiscated by the Cuban regime. Any person or company doing business in Cuba should heed this announcement. . . .

Today we are holding the Cuban Government accountable for seizing American assets. We are helping those whom the regime has robbed get compensation or their rightful property. And we're advancing human rights and democracy on behalf of the Cuban people.

Source: Remarks to the Press, United States Department of State, Michael R. Pompeo, Secretary of State, April 17, 2019, https://www.state.gov/remarks-to-the-press-11.

CUBAN GOVERNMENT DECLARATION ON VENEZUELA
(JANUARY 24, 2019)

The Revolutionary Government of the Republic of Cuba condemns and strongly rejects the attempt to impose by means of a coup d'état a puppet government at the service of the United States in the Bolivarian Republic of Venezuela. It also expresses its total and complete solidarity with the constitutional government headed by Nicolás Maduro Moros.

The true objectives of these actions against Venezuela are to control the vast resources of this sister nation, and destroy the value of its example as a country that has sought to emancipate people, and defend both the dignity and independence of Our Latin America.

As President Miguel Díaz-Canel Bermúdez has expressed: "The sovereignty of our peoples is at a decisive point, and a great deal depends upon how we react to the situation in Venezuela. Supporting the legitimate right of our sister nation to define its own destiny is to defend the dignity of us all. . . .

The actions of a group of countries and the shameful role of the OAS constitute a new and desperate attempt to apply a failed policy of regime change—a process which has not been successful because of the unbreakable resistance of the Venezuelan people, and its wish to defend national sovereignty."

Source: "Declaración del Gobierno Revolucionario de Cuba sobre intento de Golpe de Estado en Venezuela," January 24, 2019, http://www.cubadebate. cu/noticias/2019/01/24/declaracion-del-gobierno-revolucionario-de-cuba-sobre-intento-de-golpe-de-estado-en-venezuela.

CUBAN GOVERNMENT EXPLANATIONS FOR POSTPONING THE DECISION ON SAME-SEX MARRIAGE

National Assembly of Cuba (December 18, 2018)

@AsambleaCuba

#Homero The Organizing Commission proposes postponing the concept of marriage. In other words this definition should result from the Constitutional Project as a way of respecting all opinions. Marriage is a social and legal institution. The law will define the remaining elements.

@DiazCanelB

National Assembly@Assembly (December 18, 2018)

In the Family Code we need to establish who can be partners in marriage. A Popular Consultation and Referendum will take place within a period of two years following a temporary proposal put forward within the project. #ReformaConstitucional@DiazCanelB

EVANGELICAL PROTESTANT CHURCHES' REACTION TO THE PROPOSAL FOR SAME-SEX MARRIAGE

Havana, November 13, 2018

To: Organizing Committee of the Constitutional Advisory Commission, Central Committee, Communist Party of Cuba

From: Presidents and representatives of the Evangelical Church

We are pleased to officially present 179,809 signatures of people who are members of the following churches: Iglesia Pentecostal Asamblea de Dios, Iglesia Metodista en Cuba, Convención Bautista Oriental, Liga Evangélica de Cuba, Iglesia de Dios del Evangelio Completo, Sociedad Misionera Hermanos en Cristo, Iglesia Evangélica Independiente, Iglesia de Dios en Cuba, Iglesia Apostólica Fuego y Dinámica del Espíritu Santo, Iglesia Evangélica Libre, Iglesia Católica, Comunidad Cristiana e Iglesia Pentecostal Luz del Mundo.

The signatories support proposal 13 issued by the Evangelical Churches [. . .] and presented at the National Assembly of Poder Popular on October 4, 2018, with a copy to the Organizing Committee of the Constitutional Advisory Committee, as well as the Government Office Dealing with Religious Matters of the Central Committee of the Communist Party of Cuba, and the Ministry of Justice.

Concerning Modifications to Article 68, paragraph 192: "Matrimony is the voluntary union between <u>two people</u> who are legally able to do so, with the objective of sharing life together, and is based upon the absolute equality of

duties and rights of the partners, who are obliged to share the upkeep of their
home and development and upkeep of children, working together in such a
way that this conforms with the development of social activities."

We propose that instead we should retain the principle found in the current Constitution:

"Matrimony is the voluntary union of a man and a woman, who are legally able to do so, with the objective of sharing life together."

REMARKS BY NATIONAL SECURITY ADVISOR JOHN R. BOLTON ON THE POLICY OF THE UNITED STATES TOWARD CUBA (NOVEMBER 2, 2018)

Miami Dade College, Miami, FL

AMB. BOLTON: . . . . [T]oday, in this Hemisphere, we are also confronted once again with the destructive forces of oppression, socialism, and totalitarianism. In Cuba, Venezuela, and Nicaragua, we see the perils of poisonous ideologies left unchecked, and the dangers of domination and suppression.

This afternoon, I am here to deliver a clear message from the President of the United States on our policy toward these three regimes. Under this administration, we will no longer appease dictators and despots near our shores. We will not reward firing squads, torturers, and murderers.

We will champion the independence and liberty of our neighbors. And this President, and his entire administration, will stand with the freedom fighters.

The Troika of Tyranny in this Hemisphere—Cuba, Venezuela, and Nicaragua—has finally met its match.

And as I say, there is no better place to deliver this message than right here in Miami, at the Freedom Tower. Miami is home to countless Americans, who fled the prisons and death squads of the Castro regime in Cuba, the murderous dictatorships of Chavez and Maduro in Venezuela, and the horrific violence of the 1980s and today under the brutal reign of the Ortegas in Nicaragua. . . .

Everyone here today understands this fundamental truth. There is no glamor in gulags and labor camps, in death squads and propaganda machines, in mass executions and the sound of terrorizing screams from the depths of the world's most notorious prisons. These are the true consequences of socialism and communism. This is the price of freedom's extinguished flame.

As the President has said, the problems we see in Latin America today have not emerged because socialism has been implemented poorly. On the contrary, the Cuban, Venezuelan, and Nicaraguan people suffer in misery because socialism has been implemented effectively. In Cuba, a brutal dictatorship under the façade of a new figurehead continues to frustrate democratic aspirations, and jail and torture opponents. In Venezuela and Nicaragua, desperate autocratic leaders, hell-bent on maintaining their grip on power, have joined their Cuban counterparts in the same oppressive behavior of unjust imprisonment, torture, and murder.

This Troika of Tyranny, this triangle of terror stretching from Havana to Caracas to Managua, is the cause of immense human suffering, the impetus of enormous regional instability, and the genesis of a sordid cradle of communism in the Western Hemisphere. Under President Trump, the United States is taking direct action against all three regimes to defend the rule of law, liberty, and basic human decency in our region. As the President has repeatedly made clear, America's security and prosperity benefits when freedom thrives near our shores. . . .

Our policy is transparent for the American people and the world to see. It is encapsulated in National Security Presidential Memorandum-5, entitled "Strengthening the Policy of the United States Toward Cuba." And, in June of last year, President Trump came right here to Miami to outline this administration's new policy and to announce the cancellation of the last administration's one-sided and misguided deal with the Cuban regime. As the President said then, the United States will not prop up a military monopoly that abuses the citizens of Cuba.

Under our approach, the United States is enforcing U.S. law to maintain sanctions until, among other things, all political prisoners are freed, freedoms of assembly and expression are respected, all political parties are legalized, and free and internationally supervised elections are scheduled.

Importantly, our policy includes concrete actions to prevent American dollars from reaching the Cuban military, security, and intelligence services.

Today, I want to emphasize that that national security directive was just the beginning of our effort to pressure the Cuban regime. Since its release, we have been tightening sanctions against the Cuban military and intelligence services, including their holding companies, and closing loopholes in our sanctions resolutions. . . .

In response to the vicious attacks on Embassy Havana, we have also scaled back our embassy personnel in Cuba. This President will not allow our diplomats to be targeted with impunity. And we will not excuse those who harm our highest representatives abroad by falsely invoking videos, or concocting some other absurd pretext for their suffering. . . .

We will only engage with a Cuban government that is willing to undertake necessary and tangible reforms—a government that respects the interests of the Cuban people.

In Venezuela, the United States is acting against the dictator Maduro, who uses the same oppressive tactics that have been employed in Cuba for decades. . . .

The Venezuelan regime's repression is of course enabled by the Cuban dictatorship. The United States calls on all nations in the region to face this obvious truth, and let the Cuban regime know that it will be held responsible for the continued oppression in Venezuela. . . .

Finally, in Nicaragua, the United States continues to condemn the Ortega regime's violence and repression against its citizens and opposition members. Ortega and his allies have completely eroded democratic institutions, stifled free speech, and imposed a policy of jail, exile, or death for political opponents. . . .

This behavior is unacceptable anywhere, and especially in the Western Hemisphere. Free, fair, and early elections must be held in Nicaragua, and democracy must be restored to the Nicaraguan people. . . .

The Troika of Tyranny in this Hemisphere will not endure forever. . . .

We know their day of reckoning awaits. We see its origins in the brave Ladies in White, who courageously take to the streets to defend their families and all of Cuba. We feel its shiver in the crowd around the flag-draped coffin of fifteen-year-old Orlando Cordoba, killed in a peaceful protest in Nicaragua. We hear its echo in the piercing chants outside of a Venezuelan military base: "Libertad! Libertad! Libertad!". . . .

The Troika will crumble. The people will triumph. And, the righteous flame of freedom will burn brightly again in this Hemisphere.

Source: White House, November 2, 2018, https://www.whitehouse.gov/briefings-statements/remarks-national-security-advisor-ambassador-john-r-bolton-administrations-policies-latin-america.

DECREE NO. 349/2018 ON VIOLATIONS OF REGULATIONS DEALING WITH CULTURAL POLICY AND ARTISTIC SERVICES (APRIL 20, 2018)

ARTICLE 1. We consider violations of this official Decree to be the conduct of anybody which goes against the current legal norms and regulations in matters of cultural policy and artistic services, as established by the Ministry of Culture with reference to the different artistic performances and services, in both public and private locations.

ARTICLE 2.1 The following are examples of violations of acceptable artistic practices:

  a. Anybody who approves or allows artistic services, or provides the means—either on their own property or elsewhere to which they have authority—without first obtaining approval and legal contract from the cultural institution responsible for allowing the use of the facilities;
  b. Anybody who provides payment, or allows payment to be made, for an individual artist or group, without said services being contracted by the appropriate cultural institution responsible for approving such practices;
  c. Any individual artist, or representative of a group of artists, who provides artistic services without receiving authorization from the cultural institution to which they belong;
  d. Any individual or group who carries out the duties of a cultural institution without authorization of said institution; and
  e. Anybody who provides a cultural service without being authorized to undertake such activities in an artistic occupation.

ARTICLE 3.1 A violation will occur when any of the following occur within any audiovisual cultural activity:

  a. Use of patriotic symbols which contravene current legislation;
  b. Pornography;
  c. Violence;
  d. Sexist, vulgar or obscene language;
  e. Any discrimination based upon skin color, sexual orientation, disability, and anything else which offends human dignity;
  f. Anything which is offensive to the development of children or adolescents;
  g. Any content which infringes upon the legal provisions which regulate the normal development of our society in cultural matters [. . .]

INAUGURAL SPEECH BY MIGUEL DÍAZ-CANEL BERMÚDEZ, PRESIDENT OF CUBA'S COUNCILS OF STATE AND MINISTERS

In the Constituent Session of the National Assembly of People's Power 9th Legislature, April 19, 2018.

I come to speak on behalf of all Cubans, who today begin a new mandate at the service of a nation whose history makes us proud; not only those born in this land, but millions of children of America and the world that love and respect it as their own. I do so with all the responsibility that an act of this nature entails and with the awareness that we are not inaugurating just another legislature. Martí said that "pompous words are unnecessary to speak of sublime men." And this is the case now, when I fulfill, with honor and emotion, the mandate of our people to dedicate the first thought to the historic generation that, with exemplary dedication and humility, accompanies us in this hour of pressing challenges in which Cuba expects that we be like them, capable of victoriously fighting all the battles that await us. . . .

More than half a century of slander and dark invitations to generational rupture and discouragement in the face of difficulties, have not been able to tear down the columns of the temple of our faith: the Revolution of Fidel and the Centennial Generation of Martí continues in its 60th year with the dignity of its founders intact and ennobled by having been able to do in each moment what each moment demanded. . . .

Compatriots: Two years ago today, in the closure of the 7th Party Congress, the Army General told us that his generation would hand over, and I quote: "the banners of the Revolution and Socialism to new leaders, without the slightest trace of sadness or pessimism, with the pride of having fulfilled one's duty, convinced that they will be able to continue and magnify the Revolution's work, to which great effort was devoted, and life itself for many generations of compatriots."

This means, among many reasons, that the mandate given by the people to this Legislature is to provide continuity to the Cuban Revolution at a crucial historic moment, which will be marked by all that we manage to advance in the updating of the economic and social model, perfecting and strengthening our work in all spheres of national life.

I assume the responsibility for which I have been elected with the conviction that all Cuban revolutionaries, from the position we occupy, based on the work we do, from any post or trench of the socialist homeland, will be faithful to the exemplary legacy of the Comandante en Jefe Fidel Castro Ruz, historic leader of our Revolution, and also to the example, the courage and the teachings of Army General Raúl Castro Ruz, current leader of the revolutionary process. . . .

Fidel and Raúl, bound by blood, ideals, and struggle, show us the meaning of the word brother in its highest degree, so valued in the emotional ties of national identity. Much more. They, along with the men and women who brought the Revolution to this point, offer us the key to a new siblinghood, forged in the resistance and the shared battles that transformed us into compañeras and compañeros. Unity, so necessary while the nation was being forged, is since 1959 its most valuable and sacred strength; that has become extraordinary and invulnerable in the core of our only Party, which was not born of the rupture or splitting of others, but of the integration of all those that set out to build a better country.

For us it is totally clear that only the Communist Party of Cuba, the superior leading force of society and the state, guarantees the unity of the Cuban nation and is the worthy heir to the confidence placed in their leaders by the people, as compañero Raúl Castro Ruz stated in his speech on the 45th anniversary of the creation of the Western Army, on June 14, 2006. . . .

I am aware of the concerns and expectations that a moment such as this naturally raises, but we have the strength, intelligence and wisdom of the people; the experience and leadership of the Party; the ideas of Fidel and the presence of Raúl . . . as well as the strength, prestige, loyalty, and example of an Army founded by those who will never cease to represent the uniformed people.

Knowing popular feeling, I state to this Assembly, the supreme organ of state power, that compañero Army General Raúl Castro Ruz, as first secretary of the Communist Party of Cuba, will take the lead in the most important decisions for the present and future of the country.

We are living in a world characterized by growing threats to peace and security, interventionist wars, dangers to the survival of the human species and an unjust and exclusionary international economic order. In this context, I reaffirm that Cuban foreign policy will remain the same and reiterate that no one will be able to weaken the Revolution or crush the Cuban people, because Cuba does not make concessions essential to its sovereignty or independence, negotiate its principles or accept conditions. We will never give in to pressure or threats; the sovereign Cuban people will continue to decide the changes that need to be made.

I am aware that the task we are charged with entails an enormous responsibility to the people, which is why I call for the support of all those who occupy leadership responsibilities at different levels and in different institutions of the Revolution, but above all, I trust in the decisive support of the Cuban people, without which—and facing threats and challenges, which will always exist for a country committed to Revolution—it will be impossible for our society to successfully advance. Our management and leadership must be increasingly collective, in constant contact with the people and facilitating the participation of the population in revolutionary tasks and decision making, through broadly democratic processes which are already an insepa-rable part of national policy.

In the same way that the Revolution has never made any promises over all these years, nor will I. I am here to express my commitment to work for and ensure the fulfilment of the program that we have given ourselves as a government and a people, in the form of the Policy Guidelines of the Party and Revolution over the short, medium, and long term. Only hard, selfless and efficient work every day will lead to concrete results and achievements which will represent new victories for the homeland and socialism, without ever abandoning the combative readiness of our undefeated Revolutionary Armed Forces.

This is how we will confront the threats of our powerful imperialist neighbor. Here, there is no space for a transition that ignores or destroys so many years of struggle. In Cuba, the people have decided, that there is only room for the generations born and educated under the Revolution and the founding generation to continue to work, without bowing to pressure, with-out fear or retreat, defending our truth and motives, without renouncing our sovereignty and independence, development programs or dreams. We will always be willing to dialogue and cooperate on the basis of respect and equality, with those who are also willing to do so.

There will be no space in this legislature for those who aspire to the restoration of capitalism; this legislature will defend the Revolution and will continue perfecting socialism. . . .

In the age of communication, our adversaries have been able to lie, distort and silence our Revolutionary work. And even then they have still not been able to destroy it. We must be more creative when spreading our truth. At a time when there exist more tribunals than the open and multitudinous ones that were, at another time, the loud-speaker of the Revolution, we must learn to make more and better use of the possibilities of technology in order to inundate our truths across infinite spaces on planet internet, where today lies reign.

Let us clearly state that the Cuban Revolution continues to be olive green, and ready to take on all battles. The first being to overcome our own acts of indiscipline, mistakes and imperfections, while at the same time advancing "without haste, but without pause"—a wise warning from compañero Raúl—toward the horizon, toward the prosperity we owe ourselves and which we must achieve sooner or later, in the midst of the turmoil of a world weakened by uncertainty, injustice, violence by the powerful, and contempt for small nations and the poor majorities.

Compañeras and compañeros: On a day as symbolic as today, full of emotion and meaning, on which we have shared commitments and convic-tions, we think of Fidel, of his ideas, of his formidable, prolific, indispens-able legacy, as a way of nurturing this genuine desire to keep him among us, forever. May every fiber of our revolutionary lineage tremble when we proclaim: I am Fidel!

And we swear to defend until our last breath this "socialist and democratic Revolution of the humble, by the humble and for the humble," won for us by the historic generation fighting on the sands of Playa Girón, 57 years ago, and which now hands it over to us, undefeated and assured that we will know how to take it as far, and place it as high as they did, are doing, and will continue to do.

It is vital to state today: Homeland or death!

Socialism or death!

We will overcome!

Source: *Granma International*, April 24, 2018, http://en.granma.cu/cuba/2018-04-24/i-assume-this-responsibility-with-the-conviction-that-all-revolutionaries-will-be-loyal-to-the-exemplary-legacy-of-fidel-and-raul.

CUBAN RESPONSE TO WITHDRAWAL OF US DIPLOMATS (OCTOBER 3, 2017)

Statement by the Ministry of Foreign Affairs of the Republic of Cuba in response to recent measures taken by the Trump administration following incidents involving U.S. diplomatic personnel in Havana, October 3, 2017:

On September 29, 2017, the US Secretary of State Rex Tillerson announced the decision to significantly downscale the diplomatic staff of the US embassy in Havana and withdraw all their relatives, claiming that there had been "attacks" perpetrated against US Government officials in Cuba which have harmed their health. Once again, on October 3, the US Government, in an unwarranted act, decided that 15 officials of the Cuban Embassy in Washington should depart from the United States, claiming that the US had reduced their diplomatic staffing levels in Havana and that the Cuban Government had failed to take all appropriate steps to prevent "attacks" against them.

The Ministry of Foreign Affairs strongly protests and condemns this unfounded and unacceptable decision as well as the pretext used to justify it, for it has been asserted that the Cuban Government did not take the appropriate measures to prevent the occurrence of the alleged incidents. In the meeting that, at the proposal of the Cuban side, was held with Secretary of State Rex Tillerson, the minister of Foreign Affairs of the Republic of Cuba, Bruno Rodríguez Parrilla, warned him against the adoption of hasty decisions that were not supported by evidence; urged him not to politicize a matter of this nature and once again required the effective cooperation from the US authorities to clarify facts and conclude the investigation. . . .

Just as was expressed by the Cuban Foreign Minister to Secretary of State Tillerson on September 26, 2017, Cuba, whose diplomatic staff members have been victims in the past of attempts perpetrated against their lives, who have been murdered, disappeared, kidnapped or attacked during the performance of their duty, has seriously and strictly observed its obligations under the Geneva Convention on Diplomatic Relations of 1961 referring to the protection and integrity of diplomatic agents accredited in the country, in which it has an impeccable record.

As was informed by the Ministry on August 9 last, since February 17, 2017, when the US embassy and State Department notified the alleged occurrence of incidents against some officials of that diplomatic mission and their relatives as from November 2016, arguing that these had caused them injuries and other disorders, the Cuban authorities have acted with utmost seriousness, professionalism and immediacy to clarify this situation and opened an exhaustive and priority investigation following instructions from the top level of the Government. The measures adopted to protect the US diplomatic staff, their relatives and residences were reinforced; new expeditious communication channels were established between the US embassy and the Diplomatic Security Department and a committee of experts was created to make a comprehensive analysis of facts, which was made up by law enforcement officials, physicians and scientists.

In the face of the belated, fragmented and insufficient information supplied by the US, the Cuban authorities requested further information and clarifications from the US embassy in order to carry out a serious and profound investigation. The US embassy only delivered some data of interest on the alleged incidents after February 21, when President Raúl Castro Ruz personally reiterated to the Chargé d'Affaires of the US diplomatic mission how important it was for the competent authorities from both countries to cooperate and exchange more information.

Nevertheless, the data supplied later on continued to be lacking in the descriptions or details that would facilitate the characterization of facts or the identification of potential perpetrators, in case there were any. In the weeks that followed, in view of new reports on the alleged incidents and the scarce information that had been delivered, the Cuban authorities reiterated the need to establish an effective cooperation and asked the US authorities for more information and insisted that the occurrence of any new incident should be notified in real time, which would provide for a timely action.

Besides all of the above and in the interest of contributing to the investigation and legal process established by virtue of the Cuban Criminal Procedural Law, the US received from Cuba some requests for information as part of the inquiry procedure.

The information delivered by the US authorities led the committee of Cuban experts conclude [*sic*] that this was insufficient and that the main obstacle to clarify the incidents had been the impossibility to have direct access to the injured people and the physicians who examined them; the belated delivery of evidence and their deficient value; the absence of reliable first-hand and verifiable information and the inability to exchange with US experts who are knowledgeable about this kind of events and the technology that could have been used, despite having repeatedly stating [*sic*] this as a requirement to be able to move forward in the investigation. Only after repeated requests were conveyed to the US Government, some representatives of specialized agencies of that country finally traveled to Havana on June last, met with their Cuban counterparts and expressed their intention to cooperate in a more substantive way in the investigation of the alleged incidents. They again visited Cuba in August and September, and for the first time in more than 50 years they were allowed to work on the ground, for which they were granted all facilities, including the possibility of importing equipment, as a gesture of good will that evidenced the great interest of the Cuban government in concluding the investigation.

The Cuban authorities highly assessed the three visits made by the US specialized agencies, which have recognized the high professional level of the investigation started by Cuba and its high technical and scientific component, and which, as a preliminary result, concluded that, so far, according to the information available and the data supplied by the United States, there were [*sic*] no evidence of the occurrence of the alleged incidents or the causes and the origin of the health disorders reported by the US diplomats and their relatives. Neither has it been possible to identify potential perpetrators or persons with motivations, intentions or means to perpetrate this type of actions [*sic*]; nor was it possible to establish the presence of suspicious persons or means at the locations where such facts have been reported or in their vicinity. The Cuban authorities are not familiar with the equipment or the technology that could be used for that purpose; nor do they have information indicating their presence in the country.

The Ministry of Foreign Affairs categorically rejects any responsibility of the Cuban Government in the alleged incidents and reiterates once again that Cuba has never perpetrated, nor will it ever perpetrate attacks of any sort against diplomatic officials or their relatives, without any exception. Neither has it ever allowed nor will it ever allow its territory to be used by third parties with that purpose. . . .

The Ministry reiterates Cuba's disposition to continue fostering a serious and objective cooperation between the authorities of both countries with the purpose of clarifying these facts and conclude the investigation, for which it will be essential to count on the most effective cooperation of the US competent agencies.

Source: *Granma International*, October 3, 2017, http://en.granma.cu/cuba/2017-10-03/cuban-foreign-ministry-responds-to-latest-measures-by-trump-administration.

CONCEPTUALIZATION OF THE CUBAN SOCIAL AND ECONOMIC MODEL OF SOCIALIST DEVELOPMENT (JULY 2017, TRANSLATION BY JOHN M. KIRK)

Chapter 1: The Principles upon Which the Model and Its Principal Transformations Are Based

The Conceptualization of the updated model outlines and explains the basis for its strategic objectives, as well as the principles which underpin it, and the major transformations needed due to present-day circumstances.

The Conceptualization also serves as a guide as we advance toward the full implementation of our Vision of the Nation: independent, sovereign, socialist, democratic, prosperous and sustainable, by means of the long-term National Plan of Socio-Economic Development, and other policies.

The strategic objectives of the updating of the Model are: to guarantee the irreversible nature and continuity of our socialist system strengthening the very principles which support it, as well as the economic development and the promotion of both the level and quality of life with equity. All of this, presented along with the necessary development of the 13 ethical and political values, while rejecting selfishness, individualism, and alienating predatory consumerism.

The updated Model, in line with the present Conceptualization, is not conceived as a completed, static norm, but rather as an active outline—one which can be improved and perfected based upon the advances in the theory of socialist construction and its relationship with practical experience. . . .

The Model comprises the areas of production, distribution, exchange and consumption. It has important impacts on all areas, and can be seen as a multidimensional, integral process in which different activities, as well as social and economic sectors, intervene.

In each period the strategic economic activities are identified based upon both their significance and the impact that they have on other factors, and this process is determined as an integral component in the development of planning.

They are decisive for the sustainable nature and prosperity of the nation, as well as the education and formation in terms of values, health, science, technology and innovation, culture, social communication, defense and national security, the rational use and protection of resources and the environment, among others.

Sustainability in economic, social and environmental matters is associated with development, and requires rhythms and structures of economic growth which will ensure prosperity accompanied by social justice and equity, in harmony with the environment, as well as the rational use and conservation of natural resources, and the care and enrichment of the nation's patrimony.

In order to reach these objectives, the efficient and effective performance of the economy represents a fundamental premise which should drive the creation of the necessary material support for the distribution of wealth in a way that is socially just and equitable.

A prosperous and sustainable socialist system can be realized based upon a profound revolutionary awareness and commitment, a sense of duty, work which is carried out efficiently and effectively, the participation of workers, a high degree of motivation, the rational use and protection of resources, progress, and the application of the results learned from science, technology and innovation. . . .

1.2 The Major Transformations upon Which the Updating of the Model Are Based

These transformations have as general objectives the consolidation of our principles as well as the momentum for sustainable socio-economic development in order to increase wealth and a more just, equitable redistribution of this wealth. These will be accompanied by the necessary formation of ethical, cultural and political values of our citizens, given their leading role in the deliberate construction of a new society.

The principal transformations are:

1. To consolidate the essential role of socialist property for the entire population on the basis of the fundamental means of production, differentiating between the exercise of ownership and that of possession or administration. At the same time to recognize and diversify different forms of property and management, which are to be appropriately connected.
2. To transform in an integral fashion the System of Administration of Social and Economic Development, using a planning system as its principal component. The centralized nature is to be combined with the decentralization and autonomy that are required in intermediate and base instances, as well as the use of direct and indirect administration approaches. This implies the integral re-design of the monetary, exchange, tax, credit, price, salary and other forms of income systems of Cuban citizens. To recognize, regulate and successfully attain an adequate market system, so that the centralized administrative measures, together with macroeconomic politics and other policies, encourage the economic actors to adopt decisions in accordance with the interests of our entire society.

3. To succeed in making our painstaking efforts an essential moral value, and in addition to ensure that the application of the principle of socialist distribution (based upon quality, complexity and quantity of labor employed) will allow this to become the fundamental means of satisfying the material and spiritual needs of our citizens, including the realization of projects held by individuals, families, and collectives.
4. To improve the State, its systems, organs, and administrative methods, as the leading institution of social and economic development, coordinating and regulating the activities of all involved in the system.

This implies concentrating on the functions that are inherent to it, among which several key objectives are particularly important: to consolidate a series of universal social policies, based on the need for equity and sustainability, that are relevant in terms of health, education, security and social assistance, culture, support for physical and sports activities, and the development in both value and quality of public services; to modernize public administration; to decentralize administration at the territorial and local levels, especially at the municipal level; to apply in a more effective manner the policy of cadres at the State and Government level; to improve the system of legal principles as found in the Constitution of the Republic, ensuring the rights of citizens.

The functions of the State in social and economic matters—including those related to the government—are derived from the socialist character of the Cuban State, the principal guiding force in all social and economic facets. These functions include the development, application and improvement of State and Government policies, as well as its role in treasury matters, in passing official regulations, and in ensuring the implementation of these aspects, and their successful application.

To improve democratic participation at all levels, especially control by the people and involvement of citizens in resolving problems that affect every territory, work center or community. To obtain an effective form of social communication, with a particular emphasis on quality and appropriate access to public information.

Source: http://www.granma.cu/file/pdf/gaceta/Conceptualizaci%C3%B3n%20del%20modelo%20economico%20social%20Version%20Final.pdf.

REMARKS BY PRESIDENT TRUMP ON THE POLICY OF THE UNITED STATES TOWARD CUBA (JUNE 16, 2017)

Manuel Artime Theater, Miami, FL

THE PRESIDENT: . . . I am so thrilled to be back here with all of my friends in Little Havana. . . .

What you have built here—a vibrant culture, a thriving neighborhood, the spirit of adventure—is a testament to what a free Cuba could be. And with God's help, a free Cuba is what we will soon achieve. . . .

We are deeply honored to be joined by amazing Veterans of the Bay of Pigs. These are great people, amazing people.

I have wonderful memories from our visit during the campaign. That was some visit. That was right before the election. I guess it worked, right? Boy, Florida, as a whole, and this community supported us by tremendous margins. We appreciate it.

But including one of the big honors, and that was the honor of getting the Bay of Pigs award just before the election, and it's great to be gathered in a place named for a true hero of the Cuban people. And you know what that means. . . .

Many of you witnessed terrible crimes committed in service of a depraved ideology. You saw the dreams of generations held by captive, and just, literally, you look at what happened and what communism has done. You knew faces that disappeared, innocents locked in prisons, and believers persecuted for preaching the word of God. You watched the Women in White bruised, bloodied, and captured on their way from Mass. You have heard the chilling cries of loved ones, or the cracks of firing squads piercing through the ocean breeze. Not a good sound. . . .

The exiles and dissidents here today have witnessed communism destroy a nation, just as communism has destroyed every single nation where it has ever been tried. . . .

Last year, I promised to be a voice against repression in our region—remember, tremendous oppression—and a voice for the freedom of the Cuban people. You heard that pledge. You exercised the right you have to vote. You went out and you voted. And here I am like I promised—like I promised. . . . And now that I am your President, America will expose the crimes of the Castro regime and stand with the Cuban people in their struggle for freedom. Because we know it is best for America to have freedom in our hemisphere, whether in Cuba or Venezuela, and to have a future where the people of each country can live out their own dreams.

For nearly six decades, the Cuban people have suffered under communist domination. To this day, Cuba is ruled by the same people who killed tens of thousands of their own citizens, who sought to spread their repressive and failed ideology throughout our hemisphere, and who once tried to host ene-my nuclear weapons 90 miles from our shores.

The Castro regime has shipped arms to North Korea and fueled chaos in Venezuela. While imprisoning innocents, it has harbored cop killers, hijack-ers, and terrorists. It has supported human trafficking, forced labor, and ex-ploitation all around the globe. This is the simple truth of the Castro regime. My administration will not hide from it, excuse it, or glamorize it. And we will never, ever be blind to it. We know what's going on and we remember what happened. . . . It's hard to think of a policy that makes less sense than the prior administration's terrible and misguided deal with the Castro re-gime. . . . They made a deal with a government that spreads violence and instability in the region and nothing they got—think of it—nothing they got—they fought for everything and we just didn't fight hard enough. But now those days are over. Now we hold the cards. We now hold the cards. The previous administration's easing of restrictions on travel and trade does not help the Cuban people—they only enrich the Cuban regime. The profits from investment and tourism flow directly to the military. The regime takes the money and owns the industry. The outcome of the last administration's executive action has been only more repression and a move to crush the peaceful, democratic movement.

Therefore, effective immediately, I am canceling the last administration's completely one-sided deal with Cuba. . . . I am announcing today a new policy, just as I promised during the campaign, and I will be signing that contract right at that table in just a moment.

Our policy will seek a much better deal for the Cuban people and for the United States of America. We do not want US dollars to prop up a military monopoly that exploits and abuses the citizens of Cuba.

Our new policy begins with strictly enforcing US law. We will not lift sanctions on the Cuban regime until all political prisoners are freed, free-doms of assembly and expression are respected, all political parties are legal-ized, and free and internationally supervised elections are scheduled. Elec-tions. We will very strongly restrict American dollars flowing to the military, security and intelligence services that are the core of [the] Castro regime. They will be restricted. We will enforce the ban on tourism. We will enforce the embargo. We will take concrete steps to ensure that investments flow directly to the people, so they can open private businesses and begin to build their country's great, great future—a country of great potential. My action today bypasses the military and the government, to help the Cuban people themselves form businesses and pursue much better lives. We will keep in place the safeguards to prevent Cubans from risking their lives to unlawful travel to the United States. . . . And we will work for the day when a new generation of leaders brings this long reign of suffering to an end. And I do believe that end is in the very near future. We challenge Cuba to come to the table with a new agreement that is in the best interests of both their people and our people and also of Cuban Americans.

To the Cuban government, I say: Put an end to the abuse of dissidents. Release the political prisoners. Stop jailing innocent people. Open yourselves to political and economic freedoms. Return the fugitives from American justice—including the return of the cop-killer Joanne Chesimard. And finally, hand over the Cuban military criminals who shot down and killed four brave members of Brothers to the Rescue who were in unarmed, small, slow civilian planes. So to the Castro regime, I repeat: The harboring of criminals and fugitives will end. You have no choice. It will end.

Any changes to the relationship between the United States and Cuba will depend on real progress toward these and the other goals, many of which I've described. When Cuba is ready to take concrete steps to these ends, we will be ready, willing, and able to come to the table to negotiate that much better deal for Cubans, for Americans. . . . Our embassy remains open in the hope that our countries can forge a much stronger and better path. America believes that free, independent, and sovereign nations are the best vehicle for human happiness, for health, for education, for safety, for everything. We all accept that all nations have the right to chart their own paths—and I'm certainly a very big believer in that—so we will respect Cuban sovereignty. But we will never turn our backs on the Cuban people. That will not happen. Over the years, a special sympathy has grown between this land of the free, and the beautiful people of that island, so close to our shores and so deeply woven into the history of our region. America has rejected the Cuban people's oppressors. They are rejected. Officially today, they are rejected. And to those people, America has become a source of strength, and our flag a symbol of hope. . . .

Source: The White House, June 16, 2017, https://www.whitehouse.gov/briefings-statements/remarks-president-trump-policy-united-states-towards-cuba.

CUBAN-US MIGRATION ACCORD (JANUARY 12, 2017) JOINT STATEMENT BETWEEN THE GOVERNMENTS OF CUBA AND THE UNITED STATES

MOTIVATED by an interest in the normalization of bilateral relations consistent with the Purposes and Principles enshrined in the Charter of the United Nations, including those related to the sovereign equality of States, settlement of international disputes by peaceful means, respect for the territorial integrity and political independence of States, respect for equal rights and self-determination of peoples, non-interference in the internal affairs of States, and promotion and encouragement of respect for human rights and fundamental freedoms for all;

ENCOURAGED by the re-establishment of diplomatic relations on July 20, 2015 based on mutual respect and the political will to strengthen bilateral relations and establish new understandings in various areas of common interest;

AWARE of the necessity to facilitate regular migration to the benefit of both countries, and to discourage irregular migration;

COMMITTED to preventing irregular migration, impeding departures from the Republic of Cuba that risk loss of human life, combating acts of violence associated with irregular migration, such as trafficking in persons and alien smuggling; and beginning the regular return of Cuban nationals, as set forth in this Joint Statement. The United States of America and the Republic of Cuba have agreed to take a major step toward the normalization of their migration relations, in order to ensure a regular, safe and orderly migration.

The Joint Communiqués dated December 14, 1984 and September 9, 1994 and the Joint Statement of May 2, 1995 remain in effect except as modified by this Joint Statement (collectively known as 'Migration Accords'). This Joint Statement is not intended to modify the Migration Accords with respect to the return of Cuban nationals intercepted at sea by the United States or the return of migrants found to have entered the Guantanamo Naval Base illegally.

In this framework, the United States of America shall henceforth end the special parole policy for Cuban nationals who reach the territory of the United States (commonly referred to as the wet foot-dry foot policy), as well as the parole program for Cuban health care professionals in third countries. The United States shall henceforth apply to all Cuban nationals, consistent with its laws and international norms, the same migration procedures and standards that are applicable to nationals of other countries, as established in this Joint Statement.

1. From the date of this Joint Statement, the United States of America, consistent with its laws and international norms, shall return to the Republic of Cuba, and the Republic of Cuba, consistent with its laws and international norms, shall receive back all Cuban nationals who after the signing of this Joint Statement are found by the competent authorities of the United States to have tried to irregularly enter or remain in that country in violation of United States law. The United States of America and the Republic of Cuba state their intention to promote changes in their respective migration laws to enable fully normalized migration relations to occur between the two countries. The United States of America and the Republic of Cuba shall apply their migration and asylum laws to nationals of the other Party avoiding selective (in other words, discriminatory) criteria and consistent with their international obligations.
2. The United States of America shall continue ensuring legal migration from the Republic of Cuba with a minimum of 20,000 persons annually.
3. The United States of America and the Republic of Cuba, determined to strongly discourage unlawful actions related to irregular migration, shall promote effective bilateral cooperation to prevent and prosecute alien smuggling and other crimes related to migration movements that threaten their national security, including the hijacking of aircraft and vessels.
4. The Republic of Cuba shall accept that individuals included in the list of 2,746 to be returned in accordance with the Joint Communiqué of December 14, 1984, may be replaced by others and returned to Cuba, provided that they are Cuban nationals who departed for the United States of America via the Port of Mariel in 1980 and were found by the competent authorities of the United States to have tried to irregularly enter or remain in that country in violation of United States law. The Parties shall agree on the specific list of these individuals and the procedure for their return.
5. The Republic of Cuba shall consider and decide on a case-by-case basis the return of other Cuban nationals presently in the United States of America who before the signing of this Joint Statement had been found by the competent authorities of the United States to have tried to irregularly enter or remain in that country in violation of United States law. The competent authorities of the United States shall focus on individuals whom the competent authorities have determined to be priorities for return. . . .

The competent authorities of the United States of America and the Republic of Cuba shall meet on a regular basis to ensure that cooperation under these Migration Accords is carried out. . . .

Source: US Department of Homeland Security, https://www.dhs.gov/sites/default/files/publications/Joint%20Statement%20FINAL%20-%20US%20alt.pdf.

CUBA–EUROPEAN UNION POLITICAL DIALOGUE AND COOPERATION AGREEMENT (MARCH 11, 2016)

Statement to the press by Federica Mogherini, High Representative of the Union for Foreign Affairs and Security Policy and Vice-President of the European Commission at the 7th Ministerial Political Dialogue session between Cuba and the European Union, March 11, 2016:

I am here to celebrate a historic step in our relations. Cuba and the European Union have concluded their negotiations for a Political Dialogue and Cooperation Agreement (PDCA).

The PDCA will mark the beginning of a new phase of the bilateral relations. This contractual arrangement is a landmark demonstration of the improved mutual trust and understanding between us. It creates a clear framework for intensified political dialogue, and a platform for developing joint action and cooperation on global matters in multinational fora. . . .

The end of negotiations and upcoming signature of the Agreement mark the end of the EU's 1996 Common Position as the Union's instrument defining its external relations with Cuba. This unilateral policy had already envisaged the perspective of a contractual arrangement and will now be superseded by the PDCA. . . .

We are excited about the prospect of turning the PDCA into reality and achieve its objectives: enhancing EU-Cuba relations, promoting dialogue and cooperation to foster sustainable development, democracy and human rights, accompanying the process of "updating" the Cuban economy and society and finding common solutions to global challenges.

During my visit, I have held with Foreign Minister Bruno Rodriguez Parrilla our second formal political dialogue meeting. . . .

We have addressed our bilateral relations, regional issues in the Cuban and EU vicinity and global matters of mutual concern, such as migration. Regarding bilateral relations, we have spoken about the situation in the EU, confronted with economic challenges, instability and violence in our closest neighborhood, the refugee crisis and the fight against terrorism. And we have also talked about the situation in Cuba, the difficult economic situation and the modernization process it is facing.

We have addressed the Cuba-US opening process, and the many opportunities and challenges involved. We agree that the US embargo is completely obsolete and outdated. Now the priorities are dialogue and cooperation, and the embargo is an obstacle which has to end. Its extraterritorial effects are illegal. The EU position is clear: we don't accept that EU companies are penalised. We will work with determination to put an end to this issue which affects economic activity and development. Both Cuba and EU will work with the US to push for an end of these measures, which cause undue harm to Cuban people and society.

Concerning international relations, we spoke about international crises, such as the Middle East, as well as issues in the America region. I congratulated Cuba for the facilitation of the Colombian peace process hosted here in Havana. We also spoke about the developments in Venezuela, where we hope for a constructive dialogue necessary to address the deteriorating political deadlock, economic and security situation. A year ago, Foreign Minister Rodríguez and I agreed on launching a dedicated Human Rights dialogue to exchange views on this important and sensitive area. We wanted to develop our mutual understanding, and sound out possibilities for cooperation. This is destined to become an important part of the new PDCA framework. . . .

During my last visit, we signed the EU's Multi-annual Indicative Programme for Cuba with an allocation of €50 million for the period of 2014–2020. This is another important EU contribution strengthening EU-Cuba relations and supporting the development of the island. The MIP underpins the economic and social modernisation strategy adopted [by] the Cuban government: a sustainable, more productive agriculture sector, a better use of key natural resources, in particular renewable energies and water, as well as an updated economic and societal model. In the meantime, a project of 8 million EUR is implemented.

We will continue our support to the tax administration, to facilitate Cuban trade with the EU and the world, but we have extended the offer of experts' exchanges to other Ministries, like the Ministries of Labor and Justice. In the energy sector, a stocktaking mission of EU experts took place in January to identify strategic areas, where EU transfer of experience and know how would have the greatest impact and leverage to boost transformation of the Cuban energy sector.

I look forward to continuing our engagement with a view to supporting Cuba's sustainable socio-economic development and ensuring better opportunities for all in Cuba.

Source: *Granma International*, March 15, 2016, http://en.granma.cu/cuba/ 2016-03-15/statement-by-federica-mogherini-on-cuba-eu-agreement.

Notes

INTRODUCTION

1. Fidel Castro continued to serve formally as first secretary of the Communist Party of Cuba until 2011.

2. Pablo Bachelet, "U.S. Policy Gives the Bush Administration Few Options in Cuba, Critics Say," *McClatchy*, August 2, 2006.

3. Julia E. Sweig, "Fidel's Final Victory," *Foreign Affairs* (January/February 2007).

4. Nelson P. Valdés, "The Revolutionary and Political Content of Fidel Castro's Charismatic Authority," in *A Contemporary Cuba Reader: Reinventing the Revolution*, ed. Philip Brenner, Marguerite Rose Jiménez, John M. Kirk, and William M. LeoGrande (Lanham, MD: Rowman & Littlefield, 2007), 27.

5. Max Weber, *The Theory of Social and Economic Organization*, trans. A. M. Henderson and Talcott Parsons (New York: Free Press, 1964)

6. The period from 1829 to 1860 also experienced significant political turmoil, especially around the question of how much authority the national government had in relation to the states. In effect, the national government's legal-institutional legitimacy—as a replacement for legitimacy based on tradition—was solidified only by the North's victory in the Civil War and the passage of the Fourteenth Amendment to the Constitution. Arthur M. Schlesinger Jr., *The Age of Jackson* (Boston: Little, Brown, 1945); David S. Reynolds, *Waking Giant: America in the Age of Jackson* (New York: HarperCollins, 2008).

7. Carlos Alzugaray Treto, "Continuity and Change in Cuba at 50: The Revolution at a Crossroads," in *A Contemporary Cuba Reader: The Revolution under Raúl Castro*, Second Edition, eds. Philip Brenner, Marguerite Rose Jiménez, John M. Kirk, and William M. Leo-Grande (Lanham, MD: Rowman & Littlefield, 2014), 40–42. See also "Speech Delivered by Raúl Castro Ruz, President of the Councils of State and Ministers, at the Close of the Inaugural Session of the Seventh Legislature of the National Assembly of People's Power," Havana, February 24, 2008, accessed November 28, 2018, http://www.cuba.cu/gobierno/rauldiscursos/2008/esp/r240208e.html.

8. Details of the 2006 to 2013 period can be found in Brenner et al., *A Contemporary Cuba Reader* (2014).

9. Yailin Orta Rivera and Norge Martínez Montero, "La vieja gran estafa," *Juventud Rebelde*, October 1, 2006, accessed November 29, 2018, http://www.juventudrebelde.cu/cuba/2006-10-01/la-vieja-gran-estafa.

10. Anita Snow, "Cuba's Raul Castro Signals More Openness to Debate of Divergent Ideas Than Brother Fidel," Associated Press International, December 21, 2006.

11. Raúl Castro, "Speech at the Celebration of the Attack on Moncada," Camaguey, July 26, 2007, accessed November 29, 2018, http://www.granma.cu/granmad/secciones/raul26/02.html.

12. Marc Frank, *Cuban Revelations: Between the Scenes in Havana* (Gainesville: University Press of Florida, 2013), 73–74.

13. Frank, *Cuban Revelations*, 74.

14. United Nations Development Program, *Human Development Report 2009* (New York: Palgrave Macmillan, 2009), 167–68.

15. Denise Blum, "Cuban Educational Reform during the 'Special Period': Dust, Ashes and Diamonds," in Brenner et al., *A Contemporary Cuba Reader* (2014), 424–27.

16. Raúl Castro Ruz, "Speech before the National Assembly," February 24, 2008, accessed November 29, 2018, http://www.cuba.cu/gobierno/rauldiscursos/2008/esp/r240208e.html.

17. "Díaz-Canel apunta a la corrupción como 'enemigo principal de la Revolución,'" EFE, May 31, 2018. https://www.efe.com/efe/america/politica/diaz-canel-apunta-a-la-corrupcion-como-enemigo-principal-de-revolucion/20000035-3634307.

18. Miguel Díaz-Canel Bermúdez, "Speech to the National Assembly," April 19, 2018, accessed July 23 2019, http://www.granma.cu/elecciones-en-cuba-2017-2018/2018-04-20/asumo-la-responsabilidad-con-la-conviccion-de-que-todos-los-revolucionarios-seremos-fieles-al-ejemplar-legado-de-fidel-y-raul-video-20-04-2018-04-04-02.

19. Raúl Castro Ruz, "Central Report to the 7th Congress of the Communist Party of Cuba," April 16, 2016, accessed July 22, 2019, http://en.granma.cu/cuba/2016-04-18/the-development-of-the-national-economy-along-with-the-struggle-for-peace-and-our-ideological-resolve-constitute-the-partys-principal-missions (Council of State transcript/*Granma International* translation).

20. *Granma*, April 19, 2018; http://en.granma.cu/cuba/2018-04-19/minute-to-minute-continuity-of-the-revolution-with-a-new-council-of-state-in-cuba; Rafael Hernández, "Cuba probable. La transición socialista y el nuevo gobierno," *Latin American Perspectives*, Political Report #1332, April 19, 2018, both accessed July 18, 2019, https://laperspectives.blogspot.com/2018/04/exclusive-cuba-probable-la-transicion.html.

21. Geoff Thale and Teresa García Castro, "Cuba's New Constitution Explained," Washington Office on Latin America, February 26, 2019, 3, accessed July 20, 2019, https://www.wola.org/analysis/cubas-new-constitution-explained.

22. Jorge Mario Sánchez Egozcue, "Challenges of Economic Restructuring in Cuba," in Brenner et al., *A Contemporary Cuba Reader* (2014), 129.

23. Ricardo Torres Pérez, "Concluding Reflections of the Current Reform Process in Cuba," in *No More Free Lunch: Reflections on the Cuban Economic Reform Process and Challenges for Transformation*, ed. Claus Brundenius and Ricardo Torres Pérez (Heidelberg: Springer, 2014), 225; Armando Nova González, "Cuban Agriculture and the Current Process of Economic Transformation," in Brenner et al., *A Contemporary Cuba Reader* (2014), 153–54.

24. Raúl Castro Ruz, "Speech at the Ninth Congress of the Young Communist League," April 4, 2010, accessed November 29, 2018, http://www.cuba.cu/gobierno/rauldiscursos/2010/ing/r030410i.html.

25. Raúl Castro Ruz, "Speech at the National Assembly," August 1, 2010, accessed November 29, 2018, http://www.cuba.cu/gobierno/rauldiscursos/2010/esp/r010810e.html.

26. Sixth Congress of the Communist Party of Cuba, "Resolution on the Guidelines of the Economic and Social Policy of the Party and the Revolution," April 18, 2011, accessed November 29, 2018, http://www.cuba.cu/gobierno/documentos/2011/ing/l160711i.html.

27. Philip Brenner and Peter Eisner, *Cuba Libre: A 500-Year Quest for Independence* (Lanham, MD: Rowman & Littlefield, 2018), 310.

28. Richard E. Feinberg, *Open for Business: Building the New Cuban Economy* (Washington, DC: Brookings Institution Press, 2016), 140.

29. Juan Triana Cordoví, "Moving from Reacting to an External Shock toward Shaping a New Conception of Cuban Socialism," in Brundenius and Torres Pérez, *No More Free Lunch*, 234.

30. Antonio F. Romero Gómez, "Economic Transformations and Institutional Changes in Cuba," in *Cuba's Economic Change in Comparative Perspective*, ed. Richard E. Feinberg and Ted Piccone (Washington, DC: Brookings, 2014), 33–34; Feinberg, *Open for Business*, 28–29.

31. Oficina Nacional de Estadística e Información, *Anuario Estadístico de Cuba 2010*, Edición 2011, table 3.5, accessed November 29, 2018, http://www.one.cu/aec2010/esp/20080618_tabla_cuadro.htm.

32. Garrett Graddy-Lovelace, "United States–Cuba Agricultural Relations and Agrarian Questions," *Journal of Agrarian Change* 18, no. 1 (January 2018): 47.

33. Romero Gómez, "Economic Transformations and Institutional Changes in Cuba," 34–35.

34. Sinan Koont, "Cuba's Recent Embrace of Agroecology: Urban and Suburban Agriculture," in Brenner et al., *A Contemporary Cuba Reader* (2014), 405–6.

35. "Cuba Claims Massive Oil Reserves," *BBC News*, October 17, 2008, accessed December 1, 2018, http://news.bbc.co.uk/2/hi/americas/7675234.stm.

36. Raúl Castro Ruz, "The Revolutionary Cuban People Will Again Rise to the Occasion: Speech to the Closing Session of the National Assembly," July 18, 2016; accessed July 18, 2019, http://en.granma.cu/cuba/2016-07-13/the-revolutionary-cuban-people-will-again-rise-to-the-occasion.

37. Communist Party of Cuba, "Seventh Congress of the Communist Party of Cuba, Resolution on the Results of Implementing the Lineamientos," April 18, 2016, accessed July 24, 2019, http://www.cubadebate.cu/especiales/2016/04/18/resolucion-sobre-resultados-de-la-implementacion-de-los-lineamientos-de-la-politica-economica-y-social-del-partido-y-la-revolucion-aprobados-en-el-vi-congreso-y-su-actualizacion-el-periodo-2016-2021.

38. William M. LeoGrande, "New US Sanctions Aim to Cripple Cuba's Economy," *World-ECR* 81 (July/August 2019), http://www.worldecr.com.

39. "China Signs Trade Deals with Cuba," *BBC News*, November 19, 2008, accessed November 30, 2018, http://news.bbc.co.uk/2/hi/americas/7733811.stm.

40. John M. Kirk, "Cuban Medical Internationalism under Raúl Castro," in Brenner et al., *A Contemporary Cuba Reader* (2014), 258.

41. Kirk, "Cuban Medical Internationalism under Raúl Castro," 251.

42. Brian Ellsworth, "Despite Obama Charm, Americas Summit Boosts US Isolation," Reuters, April 16, 2012, accessed December 1, 2018, http://www.reuters.com/article/us-americas-summit-obama-idUSBRE83F0UD20120416.

43. William M. LeoGrande and Peter Kornbluh, *Back Channel to Cuba: The Hidden History of Negotiations between Washington and Havana* (Chapel Hill: University of North Carolina Press, 2015), Epilogue.

44. US Department of Commerce, Census Bureau, "Foreign Trade: Trade in Goods with Cuba," accessed December 3, 2018, https://www.census.gov/foreign-trade/balance/c2390.html.

45. Philip Brenner and Soraya M. Castro Mariño, "Untying the Knot: The Possibility of a Respectful Dialogue between Cuba and the United States," in Brenner et al., *A Contemporary Cuba Reader* (2014), 278.

46. For example, see Charlene Barshefsky and James T. Hill, chairs, *US-Latin America Relations: A New Direction for a New Reality*, Independent Task Force Report No. 60 (New York: Council on Foreign Relations, May 2008), accessed December 3, 2018, http://www.cfr.org/mexico/us-latin-america-relations/p16279.

47. Victoria Burnett and Frances Robles, "Cuba-U.S. Ties Being Strained as Doctors Flee," *New York Times*, December 20, 2015, 1.

48. Fulton Armstrong, "Time to Clean Up US Regime-Change Programs in Cuba," *Miami Herald*, December 26, 2011.

49. Josefina Vidal Ferreiro, "Press Conference," December 5, 2012, accessed December 1, 2018, http://www.minrex.gob.cu/en/press-conference-josefina-vidal-ferreiro-head-united-states-division-cuban-chancery-international.

50. Desmond Butler, "USAID Contractor Work in Cuba Detailed," Associated Press, February 12, 2012.

51. LeoGrande and Kornbluh, *Back Channel to Cuba*, 387–94.

52. US Department of State, "Country Reports on Human Rights Practices for 2012, Cuba," April 19, 2013, accessed December 1, 2018, http://www.state.gov/j/drl/rls/hrrpt/humanrightsreport/index.htm?year=2012&dlid=204441.

53. Barack Obama, "Remarks by the President at a DSCC Fundraising Reception," November 8, 2013, accessed July 24, 2019, http://www.whitehouse.gov/the-press-office/2013/11/08/remarks-president-dscc-fundraising-reception-0.

54. Randel Swanson et al., "Neurological Manifestations among US Government Personnel Reporting Directional Audible and Sensory Phenomena in Havana, Cuba," *Journal of the American Medical Association* 319, no. 1 (2018): 1069–1176.

55. Dan Hurley, "Was It an Invisible Attack on U.S. Diplomats, or Something Stranger?" *New York Times Magazine*, May 19, 2019.

56. Michael J. Bustamante and Julia E. Sweig, "Cuban Public Diplomacy," in Brenner et al., *A Contemporary Cuba Reader* (2014), 269.

57. Tom Long, *Latin America Confronts the United States: Asymmetry and Influence* (New York: Cambridge University Press, 2015), 224.

58. Sandra Levinson, "Nationhood and Identity in Contemporary Cuban Art," in Brenner et al., *A Contemporary Cuba Reader* (2014), 340.

59. Orlando Márquez Hidalgo, "The Role of the Catholic Church in Cuba Today," The Brookings Institution, July 29, 2013. Uncorrected transcript, https://www.brookings.edu/wp-content/uploads/2013/07/20130729_cuba_catholic_church_transcript.pdf.

60. "Cuba y su diáspora: Partes inseparables de una misma nación," *Espacio Laical* 28 (October–December 2011), http://www.espaciolaical.org/contens/28/3247.pdf; "Propuestas para una refundación de las presna cubana," *Espacio Laical* 33 (January–March 2013), accessed July 15, 2019, http://www.espaciolaical.org/contens/33/3651.pdf.

61. Rafael Hernández, "Intellectuals, Civil Society, and Political Power," *Social Research: An International Quarterly* 84, no. 2 (Summer 2017): 415.

62. Teresa García Castro and Philip Brenner, "Cuba 2017: The End of an Era," *Revista de Ciencia Política* 38, no. 2 (2018): 269–270, accessed July 10, 2019, http://www.revistacienciapolitica.cl/index.php/rcp/article/view/948/600.

63. Nancy Scola, "Only 5 Percent of Cubans Can Get on the Same Internet Americans Do. That Could Soon Change," *Washington Post*, December 17, 2014, accessed July 25, 2019, https://goo.gl/x1Pxye.

64. International Telecommunications Union 2019, "Percentage of Individuals Using the Internet," accessed July 25, 2019, https://www.itu.int/en/ITU-D/Statistics/Documents/statistics/2019/Individuals_Internet_2000-2018_Jun2019.xls.

65. Antonio García Martínez, "Inside Cuba's DIY Internet Revolution," *Wired*, August 2017, accessed July 18, 2019, https://www.wired.com/2017/07/inside-cubas-diy-internet-revolution.

66. Accessed July 18, 2019, http://paquetedecuba.com.

67. Ann Marie Stock, "Zooming In: Making and Marketing Films in Twenty-First-Century Cuba," in Brenner et al., *A Contemporary Cuba Reader* (2014), 351–53.

68. Margot Olavarria, "Rap and Revolution: Hip-Hop Comes to Cuba," in Brenner et al., *A Contemporary Cuba Reader* (2007), 367.

69. Carlos Varela, "Two Songs," in Brenner et al., *A Contemporary Cuba Reader* (2014), 327.

70. Andrea Rodríguez, "AP Exclusive: Cuba Softens New Law on Artistic Expression," Associated Press, December 5, 2018, accessed July 26, 2019, https://www.apnews.com/f618c920e5a74d0b82a6c2cbb8184931.

71. Hope Bastian, *Everyday Adjustments in Havana: Economic Reforms, Mobility, and Emerging Inequalities* (Lanham, MD: Lexington Books, 2018).

72. Katrin Hansing, "Race and Inequality in the New Cuba: Reasons, Dynamics, and Manifestations," *Social Research: An International Quarterly* 84, no. 2 (Summer 2017): 331.

73. Sujartha Fernandes, "Afro-Cuban Activists Fight Racism between Two Fires," *The Nation*, May 24, 2016, accessed December 3, 2018, http://www.thenation.com/article/afro-cuban-activists-fight-racism-between-two-fires.

74. Jon Lee Anderson, "Cuba's Film Godfather," *The New Yorker*, April 24, 2013.

75. Emily J. Kirk, "Setting the Agenda for Cuban Sexuality: The Role of Cuba's Cenesex," *Canadian Journal of Latin American and Caribbean Studies* 36, no. 72 (2011). Also see Jon Alpert and Saul Landau, producers, *Mariela Castro's March: Cuba's LGBT Revolution*, re-

leased November 28, 2016, HBO, accessed December 3, 2018, https://www.hbo.com/documentaries.mariela-castros-march-cubas-lgbt-revolution.

76. Lydia Smith, "Inside Cuba's LGBT Revolution: How the Island's Attitudes to Sexuality and Gender Were Transformed," *The Independent*, January 4, 2018, accessed December 3, 2018, http://www.independent.co.uk/news/world/americas/cuba-lgbt-revolution-gay-lesbian-transgender-rights-havana-raul-castro-a8122591.html.

77. Nelson Acosta and Sarah Marsh, "In Rare Campaign for Cuba, Churches Advocate against Gay Marriage," Reuters, October 16, 2018, accessed July 31, 2019, https://www.reuters.com/article/us-cuba-constitution/in-rare-campaign-for-cuba-churches-advocate-against-gay-marriage-idUSKCN1MQ2N7.

1. POLITICS

1. Raúl Castro, "Speech during the Closing Ceremony of the Sixth Session of the Seventh Legislature of the National People's Power Assembly," December 18, 2010, http://www.cuba.cu/gobierno/rauldiscursos/2010/ing/r181210i.html.

2. Fidel Castro, "The Cuban People Will Overcome," *Granma*, April 20, 2016, http://en.granma.cu/cuba/2016-04-20/fidel-castro-the-cuban-people-will-overcome.

3. Raúl Castro, "The Development of the National Economy, along with the Struggle for Peace, and Our Ideological Resolve, Constitute the Party's Principal Missions," *Granma*, April 18, 2016, http://en.granma.cu/cuba/2016-04-18/the-development-of-the-national-economy-along-with-the-struggle-for-peace-and-our-ideological-resolve-constitute-the-partys-principal-missions.

4. *Granma* staff, "New Central Committee Elected," *Granma*, April 21, 2016, http://en.granma.cu/cuba/2016-04-21/new-central-committee-elected.

5. William M. LeoGrande, "Updating the Party: Cuba's New (and Not So New) Leaders," *Huffington Post*, April 23, 2016, https://www.huffingtonpost.com/william-m-leogrande/updating-the-party-cubas_b_9766014.html.

6. Partido Comunista de Cuba, *Lineamientos de la Política Económica y Social del Partido y la Revolución*, April 18, 2011, http://www.granma.cu/file/pdf/gaceta/Lineamientos%202016-2021%20Versi%C3%B3n%20Final.pdf.

7. Castro, "The Development of the National Economy."

8. Partido Comunista de Cuba, *Conceptualización del modelo económico y social cubano de desarrollo socialista*, no date, released June 15, 2016, http://www.granma.cu/file/pdf/gaceta/Conceptualizaci%C3%B3n%20del%20modelo%20economico%20social%20Version%20Final.pdf.

9. *Granma* news staff, "Party Congress Less Than a Month Away." *Granma*, March 28, 2016, http://en.granma.cu/cuba/2016-03-28/party-congress-less-than-a-month-away.

10. See, for example, the open letter sent to Castro by prominent journalist and LGBTQ rights activist Francisco Rodríguez Cruz and posted on his blog. Francisco Rodríguez Cruz, "Carta abierta a Raúl Castro o Aplazar hasta julio el VII Congreso del Partido," Paquitoeldecuba, March 28, 2016, https://paquitoeldecuba.com/2016/03/28/carta-abierta-a-raul-castro-o-aplazar-hasta-julio-el-vii-congreso-del-partido.

11. Andrea Rodríguez and Michael Weissenstein, "Unusual Dissent Erupts inside Cuban Communist Party," Associated Press, March 30, 2016, https://apnews.com/c2c101105baf43ff90e4f0ed88b3bd1a.

12. Raúl Castro, "The Construction of a Prosperous, Sustainable Socialism in Cuba Demands That the Principles of Justice and Equality, Which Have Served as the Revolution's Foundation, Be Preserved," *Granma*, April 29, 2016, http://en.granma.cu/cuba/2016-04-29/the-construction-of-a-prosperous-sustainable-socialism-in-cuba-demands-that-the-principles-of-justice-and-equality-which-have-served-as-the-revolutions-foundation-be-preserved.

13. Fidel Castro, "Speech Delivered at the Commemoration of the 60th Anniversary of His Admission to University of Havana, in the Aula Magna of the University of Havana, on November 17, 2005," http://www.cuba.cu/gobierno/discursos/2005/ing/f171105i.html.

14. Castro, "The Development of the National Economy."

15. Raúl Castro, "Fidel, Undefeated, Has Left Us, but His Spirit of Struggle Will Permanently Remain in the Conscience of All Revolutionaries," *Granma*, December 28, 2016, http://en.granma.cu/cuba/2016-12-28/fidel-undefeated-has-left-us-but-his-spirit-of-struggle-will-permanently-remain-in-the-conscience-of-all-revolutionaries.

16. Sarah Marsh, "Cuba Says Wants to Speed Up Foreign Investment Drive," Reuters, October 31, 2016, https://www.reuters.com/article/us-cuba-tradefair/cuba-says-wants-to-speed-up-foreign-investment-drive-idUSKBN12W582.

17. Castro, "Fidel, Undefeated, Has Left us."

18. *Granma* staff, "Raúl: We Are Not Going Back, nor Will We Go Back, to Capitalism, This Is Totally Ruled Out," *Granma*, December 28, 2016, http://en.granma.cu/cuba/2016-12-28/raul-we-are-not-going-back-nor-will-we-go-back-to-capitalism-this-is-totally-ruled-out.

19. Damien Cave, "Cuba's Reward for the Dutiful: Gated Housing," *New York Times*, February 11, 2014, https://www.nytimes.com/2014/02/12/world/americas/cubas-reward-for-the-dutiful-gated-housing.html.

20. Raúl Castro, "We Will Continue to Advance along the Path Freely Chosen by Our People," *Granma*, July 17, 2017, http://en.granma.cu/cuba/2017-07-17/we-will-continue-to-advance-along-the-path-freely-chosen-by-our-people.

21. Nora Gámez Torres, "Fear Is Driving Raúl Castro to Punish Cuba's New Entrepreneurial Class, Experts Say," *Miami Herald*, August 2, 2017, http://www.miamiherald.com/news/nation-world/world/americas/cuba/article165075352.html.

22. Ricardo Torres, "We've Been Here Before," *Progreso Weekly*, August 1, 2017, https://progresoweekly.us/weve-been-here-before.

23. Sarah Marsh, "Cuba Imposes Tighter Controls on Nascent Private Sector," Reuters, July 10, 2018, https://www.reuters.com/article/us-cuba-economy/cuba-imposes-tighter-controls-on-nascent-private-sector-idUSKBN1K00XF.

24. Nora Gámez Torres, "Cuba Has 'Largest Pool of Untapped IT Talent in the Americas,'" *Miami Herald*, February 27, 2017, https://www.miamiherald.com/news/nation-world/world/americas/cuba/article135249259.html.

25. William M. LeoGrande, "Is Cuba's Vision of Market Socialism Sustainable?" *World Politics Review*, July 31, 2018, https://www.worldpoliticsreview.com/articles/25312/is-cuba-s-vision-of-market-socialism-sustainable.

26. Leticia Martínez Hernández, "Legal Norms Governing Self-Employment Modified," *Granma*, December 6, 2018.

27. Mimi Whitefield, "A New Law That Cuban Artists and Performers Say Amounts to State Censorship Takes Effect," *Miami Herald*, December 7, 2018.

28. Archibald R. M. Ritter, "Economic Illegalities and the Underground Economy in Cuba," *Focal*, RFC-06-01, March 2006.

29. Bendixen and Amandi International, *National Survey of Cubans Living in Cuba, April 2015*, http://bendixenandamandi.com/wp-content/uploads/2017/01/Cuba-Final-4.7.15-Web.pdf.

30. NORC, *A Rare Look inside Cuban Society: A New Survey of Cuban Public Opinion* (NORC, University of Chicago, 2017), http://www.norc.org/Research/Projects/Pages/survey-of-cuban-public-opinion.aspx.

31. Lillian Guerra, *Visions of Power in Cuba: Revolution, Redemption and Resistance, 1959–1971* (Chapel Hill: University of North Carolina Press, 2012).

32. Marc Frank, "In a Reversal, Cuba Tries Price Controls to Tame Food Inflation," Reuters, January 20, 2016, https://www.reuters.com/article/us-cuba-reforms-idUSKCN0UY2BD.

33. Jorge I. Domínguez, "Can Cuban Rulers Rule?" *Cuba in Transition 22*, Papers and Proceedings of the Twenty-Second Annual Meeting Association for the Study of the Cuban Economy, Miami, Florida, August 2–4, 2012, https://www.ascecuba.org/asce_proceedings/can-cuban-rulers-rule-cuba.

34. Michael Lipsky, *Street-Level Bureaucracy* (Thousand Oaks, CA: Sage, 2010).

35. Alejandro Ramírez Anderson, *Canción de Barrio*, 2014, https://www.youtube.com/watch?v=2FczuWyxfMM.

36. Bendixen and Amandi International, *National Survey of Cubans Living in Cuba*.

37. Castro, "The Development of the National Economy."

38. Anthony Boadle, "Raul Castro Calls for More Policy Debate in Cuba," *Washington Post*, December 20, 2006, http://www.washingtonpost.com/wp-dyn/content/article/2006/12/20/AR2006122001825_pf.html.

39. Raúl Castro, "Lo que nos corresponde es promover la mayor democracia en nuestra sociedad, empezando por dar el ejemplo dentro de las filas del Partido," *Granma*, January 29, 2012, http://www.granma.cu/discursos-raul/2012-01-29/lo-que-nos-corresponde-es-promover-la-mayor-democracia-en-nuestra-sociedad-empezando-por-dar-el-ejemplo-dentro-de-las-filas-del-partido.

40. Cristina Abellan Matamoros, "Cubans Now Allowed to Access the Internet from Their Own Homes, but at What Price?" *EuroNews*, July 29, 2019, https://www.euronews.com/2019/07/29/cubans-now-allowed-to-access-the-internet-from-their-own-homes-but-at-what-price.

41. Ted A. Henken and Sjammevan der Voort, "From Cyberspace to Public Space? The Emergent Blogosphere and Cuban Civil Society," in *A Contemporary Cuba Reader: The Revolution under Raúl Castro*, eds. Philip Brenner, Marguerite Rose Jimenez, John Kirk, and William M. LeoGrande (Lanham, MD: Rowman & Littlefield, 2015), 99–110.

42. Kim Wall, "Cuba: The Weekly Package," *Harper's*, June 19, 2017, https://pulitzercenter.org/reporting/cuba-weekly-package.

43. "U.S. State Department Creates Cuba Internet Task Force," Reuters, January 23, 2018, https://www.reuters.com/article/us-cuba-usa-internet/u-s-state-department-creates-cuba-internet-task-force-idUSKBN1FD06V.

44. Samuel Farber, "What's Behind the Ongoing Controversy about 'Centrism' in Cuba?" *Havana Times*, September 14, 2017, https://havanatimes.org/?p=127288.

45. José Raúl Concepción, "Is It Possible to Meld the Best of Capitalism and Socialism?" *Granma*, July 10, 2017, http://en.granma.cu/cuba/2017-07-10/is-it-possible-to-meld-the-best-of-capitalism-and-socialism.

46. Silvio Rodríguez, "Silvio y el izquierdismo infantil," July 6, 2017, Cartas desde Cuba blog, http://cartasdesdecuba.com/silvio-y-el-izquierdismo-infantil.

47. Raúl Castro, "The Communist Party Will Resolutely Support and Back the New President," *Granma*, April 20, 2018, http://en.granma.cu/cuba/2018-04-20/the-communist-party-will-resolutely-support-and-back-the-new-president.

48. Miguel Díaz-Canel, "I Assume This Responsibility with the Conviction That All Revolutionaries Will Be Loyal to the Exemplary Legacy of Fidel and Raúl," *Granma*, April 19, 2018, http://en.granma.cu/cuba/2018-04-24/i-assume-this-responsibility-with-the-conviction-that-all-revolutionaries-will-be-loyal-to-the-exemplary-legacy-of-fidel-and-raul.

49. Sarah Marsh, "Cuba's President, Steeped in Era of Hours-Long Lectures, Turns to Twitter," Reuters, December 18, 2018, https://uk.reuters.com/article/uk-cuba-internet-president/cubas-president-steeped-in-era-of-hours-long-lectures-turns-to-twitter-idUKKBN1OH2JZ.

50. "Díaz-Canel apunta a la corrupción como 'enemigo principal de la Revolución,'" EFE, May 31, 2018, https://www.efe.com/efe/america/politica/diaz-canel-apunta-a-la-corrupcion-como-enemigo-principal-de-revolucion/20000035-3634307.

51. Sarah Rainsford, "Miguel Díaz-Canel: The Man Tipped to Lead Cuba," *BBC News*, April 9, 2013, https://www.bbc.com/news/world-latin-america-22066591.

52. Anthony Faiola, "Castro Rule in Cuba Ends as Miguel Díaz-Canel Confirmed in Leadership Change," *Washington Post*, April 19, 2018, https://www.washingtonpost.com/world/the_americas/in-cubas-national-assembly-raul-castro-marks-last-moments-of-his-familys-rule/2018/04/18/82f82cd4-4293-11e8-b2dc-b0a403e4720a_story.html; EFE, "Vicepresidente cubano cree que impedir la difusión de información es una quimera," *América Economía*, May 6, 2013, https://www.americaeconomia.com/politica-sociedad/politica/vicepresidente-cubano-cree-que-impedir-la-difusion-de-informacion-es-una-.

53. Nora Gámez Torres, "Video Offers Rare Glimpse of Hardline Ideology from Presumed Next Leader of Cuba," *Miami Herald*, August 22, 2017, https://www.miamiherald.com/news/nation-world/world/americas/cuba/article168657017.html.

54. Miguel Díaz-Canel, "From Fidel and Raúl We Learned to Discard Useless Laments and Concentrate on Seeking Solutions," *Granma*, July 15, 2019, http://en.granma.cu/cuba/2019-07-

15/from-fidel-and-raul-we-learned-to-discard-useless-laments-and-concentrate-on-seeking-solutions-turning-challenges-into-opportunities-and-setbacks-into-victory

55. Associated Press, "Cuba Rations Staple Foods and Soap in Face of Economic Crisis," *New York Times*, May 11, 2019, https://www.nytimes.com/2019/05/11/world/americas/cuba-rationing-sanctions.html.

56. Miguel Díaz-Canel, "Díaz-Canel: 'Hablo en nombre de los agradecidos, los que enfrentamos el desafío de empujar un país,'" *Granma*, July 26, 2019, http://www.granma.cu/cuba/2019-07-26/diaz-canel-hablo-en-nombre-de-los-agradecidos-los-que-enfrentamos-el-desafio-de-empujar-un-pais-26-07-2019-09-07-59.

57. *Proyecto de Constitución de la República de Cuba*, released July 25, 2018, http://www.granma.cu/file/pdf/gaceta/2018_07_25%2021_10%20Tabloide%20Constituci%C3%B3n%20(sin%20precio)%20B&N.pdf.

58. Castro, "The Development of the National Economy."

59. Anthony Faiola and Rachelle Krygier, "Cuba Moves toward Officially Recognizing Private Property, Foreign Investment," *Washington Post*, July 21, 2018, https://www.washingtonpost.com/world/the_americas/cuba-moves-toward-striking-changes-to-officially-recognize-private-property-foreign-investment/2018/07/21/cd5c230a-8c69-11e8-9d59-dccc2c0cabcf_story.html.

60. Archibald R. M. Ritter and Ted A. Henken, *Entrepreneurial Cuba: The Changing Policy Landscape* (Boulder, CO: Lynne Rienner, 2014).

61. Mario J. Pentón, "Gay Marriage Does Not Fit in a Communist Country, Cuban Evangelicals Say," *Miami Herald*, July 8, 2018, https://www.miamiherald.com/news/nation-world/world/americas/cuba/article214496694.html.

62. Sarah Marsh, "Cuba's Draft Constitution Opens Path to Gay Marriage," Reuters, July 21, 2018, https://www.reuters.com/article/us-cuba-assembly-gaymarriage/cubas-draft-constitution-opens-path-to-gay-marriage-idUSKBN1KB0P6.

63. Sarah Marsh, "Cuba Panel Closes Door on Gay Marriage Constitutional Amendment," Reuters, December 18, 2018, https://www.reuters.com/article/us-cuba-gaymarriage/cuba-panel-closes-door-on-gay-marriage-constitutional-amendment-idUSKBN1OI00V.

64. Siobhán O'Grady, "Cuban Activists Had Their Annual Pro-LGBT Parade Ready. Then the Government Called It Off," *Washington Post*, May 11, 2019, https://www.washingtonpost.com/world/2019/05/11/cuban-activists-had-their-annual-pro-lgbt-parade-ready-then-government-called-it-off; Reuters, "Defiance and Arrests at Cuba's Gay Pride Parade," *New York Times*, May 12, 2019, https://www.nytimes.com/2019/05/12/world/americas/cuba-gay-pride-parade.html.

65. "Cuban Electoral Commission Informs Final Results of Referendum," *Prensa Latina*, https://www.plenglish.com/index.php?o=rn&id=39329&SEO=cuban-electoral-commission-informs-final-results-of-referendum.

2. CUBA'S ECONOMY

1. PCC, *Lineamientos de la Política Económica y Social del Partido y la Revolución*, VI Congress of Cuba's Communist Party (La Habana: Partido Comunist de Cuba, 2011).

2. "Actualización de los Lineamientos de la Política Económica y Social del Partido y la Revolución para el Periodo 2016–2021," Document of VII Congress of Cuba's Communist Party; "Conceptualización del Modelo Económico y Social Cubano de Desarrollo Socialista," Document of VII Congress of Cuba's Communist Party; "Plan Nacional de Desarrollo Económico y Social hasta 2030: Propuesta de Visión de la Nación, Ejes y Sectores Estratégicos," Document of VII Congress of Cuba's Communist Party (La Habana: Partido Comunista de Cuba, 2016).

3. O. E. Pérez, "La inversión extranjera directa en Cuba: Necesidad de su relanzamiento," *Economía y Desarrollo* 152, no. 2 (2012): 37–52.

4. C. Mesa-Lago and P. Vidal, "The Impact of the Global Crisis on Cuba's Economy and Social Welfare," *Journal of Latin American Studies* 42 (2009): 689–717.

5. "Conceptualización del Modelo Económico y Social Cubano de Desarrollo Socialista," Document of VII Congress of Cuba's Communist Party.

6. International Monetary Fund, "Data Mapper: Venezuela," April 2019; accessed on August 6, 2019, from https://www.imf.org/external/datamapper/NGDPD@WEO/OEMDC/ADVEC/WEOWORLD/VEN.

7. U.S. Energy Information Administration, "Venezuelan Crude Oil Production Falls to Lowest Level since January 2003," *Today in Energy*, May 20, 2019, accessed on August 6, 2019, from https://www.eia.gov/todayinenergy/detail.php?id=39532.

8. V. Hidalgo and Y. Doimeadiós, "Sostenibilidad fiscal: Prioridad en la agenda de transformaciones del modelo económico cubano," *Investigación Económica* LXXV, no. 298 (2016): 155–84.

9. R. Torres, "Updating the Cuban Economy: The First 10 Years," *Social Research: An International Quarterly* 84, no. 2 (2017): 255–75.

10. J. L. Rodríguez, *Temas*, March 29, 2018, accessed on April 9, 2019, from http://temas.cult.cu/ultimo-jueves-detalles/2778; United Nations University, *World Income Inequality Database* (WIID4), December 2018, accessed on August 6, 2019, from https://www.wider.unu.edu/project/wiid-world-income-inequality-database.

3. CUBAN FOREIGN POLICY, 2014–2019

1. See "El mejor regalo: Una sonrisa," *Cubadebate*, July 6, 2018, http://www.cubadebate.cu/noticias/2018/07/06/el-mejor-regalo-una-sonrisa. The latter figure is from "Díaz-Canel: 'Más que médicos son guardianes de la virtud humana,'" *Cubadebate*, December 3, 2018, http://www.cubadebate.cu/noticias/2018/12/03/diaz-canel-mas-que-medicos-son-guardianes-de-la-virtud-humana.

2. Dan Merica, "Trump Unveils New Restrictions on Travel, Business with Cuba," CNN, June 17, 2017, https://www.cnn.com/2017/06/16/politics/trump-cuba-policy/index.html.

3. For further information see "EU-Cuba Relations, Factsheet—European External Action Service," issued on May 7, 2018, https://eeas.europa.eu/headquarters/headquarters-homepage_en/16558/EU-Cuba%20percent20rela.

4. See the report by the European External Action Service, "Cuba and the EU," October 27, 2017, https://eeas.europa.eu/delegations/cuba_en/8106/Cub%20and%20the%20EU.

5. "Federica Mogherini Meets with the Foreign Minister of Cuba," Brussels, May 24, 2019, https://eeas.europa.eu/headquarters/headquarters-homepage/63119/federica-mogherini-meets-foreign-minister-cuba_en.

6. "Charles and Camilla Make History in Cuba," BBC, March 25, 2019, https://www.bbc.com/news/uk-47688610.

7. See the Cuban Constitution at https://www.constituteproject.org/constitution/Cuba_2019.pdf?lang=en.

8. For an analysis of the historical roots of Cuba's ties with the Global South, see Ernesto Domínguez López, "The Deep, Historical Roots of Cuban Anti-Imperialism," *Third World Quarterly* 38, no. 11 (2017): 2517–535.

9. In 1975, from his cell, Nelson Mandela commented upon the Cuban role after hearing about their arrival in Angola: "It was the first time that a country had come from another continent not to take something away, but to help Africans to achieve their freedom." Max Bearak, "Fidel Castro, African Hero," *Washington Post*, November 28, 2016.

10. Analúcia Danilevicz Pereira, "Cuba's Foreign Policy Towards Africa: Idealism or Pragmatism?" *Brazilian Journal of African Studies* 1, no. 2 (2016): 106. She notes that "Cuban involvement in the Third World was characterized by idealism and pragmatism, despite the fact that, in many moments, the *Realpolitik* expressed itself in a more powerful way than the idealist aspect" (107). She notes, for example, that African states reached 27 percent of United Nations seats and a third of non-aligned countries, a useful level of support for Cuba's support in international fora.

11. The civil war in Colombia lasted for fifty-two years, during which time an estimated 220,000 people were killed, 25,000 disappeared (and were presumed killed), and over 5 million were forced from their homes. Cuba, together with Chile, Norway, and Venezuela, supervised four years of negotiations in Havana between the Santos government and the FARC guerrilla army. After the completion of the peace talks in 2016, the FARC laid down their arms.

12. "Díaz-Canel: Grupo de Lima reitera propósitos injerencistas contra Venezuela," *Cubadebate*, April 16, 2019, http://www.cubadebate.cu/noticias/2019/04/16/diaz-canel-grupo.

13. Eugenio Martínez, Director General of the Latin America and Caribbean Section of the Ministry of Foreign Affairs, sums up the Cuban position: "It is striking that the secretary general of the OAS with his particular anti-Cuban obsession reiterates vulgar calumnies and lies about our country, and ignores so many issues of real urgency in Our [Latin] America." See "Cuba Rejects Ridiculous Anti-Cuban Spectacle Orchestrated by the OAS," *CubaNews*, February 13, 2019, http://www.cubanews.acn.cu/world/9032-cuba-rejects-ridiculous-.

14. "'Mientras los cubanos estén en Venezuela, es impensable el retorno a la democracia,' dice Luis Almagro," *Diario de Cuba*, July 12, 2019, http://www.diariodecuba.com/internacional/1562967695_47495.html.

15. Arleen Rodríguez Derivet, "Díaz-Canel llega a Venezuela, capital de la izquierda mundial en los 65 de Chávez," *Cubadebate*, July 28, 2017, http://www.cubadebate.cu/noticias/2019/07/28/diaz-canel-llega-a-venezuela-capital-de-la-izquierda-mundial-en-los-65-de-chavez.

16. Ted Piccone and Harold Trinkunas, "The Cuba-Venezuela Alliance: The Beginning of the End?," Latin America Initiative Foreign Policy at Brookings, Policy Brief, June 2014.

17. Marc Frank, "Cuban Trade with Venezuela Plunges over Two Years," Reuters, August 15, 2017, https://www.reuters.com/article/us-cuba-venezuela-trade/cuban-trade-with-venezuela-plunges-over-two years-idUSKCN1AV23C.

18. Nuria Barbosa León, "Cuba's International Health Cooperation," *Granma*, July 15, 2016, http://en.granma.cu/mundo/2016-07-15/cubas-international-health-cooperation.

19. José Manzaneda and Ivana Belén Ruiz, "Cuba: ¿Más cooperación médica que todo el 'mundo rico?'" *Cubadebate*, December 8, 2017, http://www.cubadebate.cu/opinion/2017/12/8/cuba-mas-cooperacion-medica-que-todo-el-mundo-rico-video.

20. John M. Kirk, "The Evolution of Cuban Medical Internationalism," in *Cuban Foreign Policy: Transformation under Raúl Castro*, ed. H. Michael Erisman and John M. Kirk (Lanham, MD: Rowman & Littlefield, 2018), 61.

21. For a detailed analysis of Cuba's role, see John M. Kirk, *Healthcare without Borders: Understanding Cuba's Medical Internationalism* (Gainesville: University Press of Florida, 2015).

22. See international trade figures for Cuba in the *Anuario Estadístico*, http://www.one.cu/aec2016/08%20Sector%20Externo.pdf.

23. Kenneth Rapoza, "China Has Forgiven Nearly $10 Billion in Debt. Cuba Accounts for Over Half," *Forbes*, May 29, 2019, https://www.forbes.com/sites/kenrapoza/2019/05/29/china-has-forgiven-nearly-10-billion-in-debt-cuba-accounts-for-over-half.

24. Angel Guerra Cabrera, "La exitosa gira euroasiática de Díaz-Canel (II)," *Cubadebate*, November 24, 2018, http://www.cubadebate.cu/opinion/2018/11/24/la-exitosa-gira-euroasiatica-de-diaz-canel-ii.

25. "Bruno Rodríguez: Las empresas chinas tienen las puertas abiertas en Cuba," *Cubadebate*, June 1, 2019, http://www.cubadebate.cu/especiales/2019/06/01/bruno-rodriguez-las-empresas-chinas-tienen-las-puertas-abiertas-en-cuba.

26. "Cancilleres de Rusia y Cuba se reúnen en Moscú: 'Tenemos planes positivos para el futuro en todas estas áreas,'" *Cubadebate*, May 27, 2019, http://www.cubadebate.cu/noticias/2019/05/27/cancilleres-de-rusia-y-cuba-se-reunen-en-moscu-tenemos-planes-positivos-para-el-futuro-en-todas-estas-areas. Speaking in July 2019 Lavrov made a similar point: "Respect to Title III and all the other articles in that legislation, Russia's criterion remains the same: they are illegal and go against international law. . . . The position of the international community speaks for itself," he concluded. See "Rusia y Cuba confirman excelente momento y desarrollo dinámico de relaciones bilaterales," *Cubadebate*, July 24, 2019, http://www.cubadebate.cu/noticias/2019/07/24/rusia-y-cuba-confirman-excelente-momento-y-desarrollo-dinamico-de-relaciones-bilaterales-fotos.

27. TASS Report, "Russia to Continue Boosting Military Technical and Economic Cooperation with Cuba—Lavrov," July 24, 2018, https://tass.com/politics/1070233.

28. See https://www.statista.com/statistics/388584/most-important-import-partners-of-cuba.

29. See https://www.statista.com/statistics/388599/most-important-export-partner-countries-for-cuba.

30. See "Turismo. Llegadas de visitantes internacionales," published by the Oficina Nacional de Estadística e información, http://www.one.cu/publicaciones/06turismoycomercio/llegadadevisitantes/servicios%20informativos%20No.06%20turismo%20%20Junio%202019.pdf.

31. Much of this information comes from Sarah Marsh and Nelson Acosta, "Cuba Boosts Trade with Cold War Ally Russia as U.S. Disengages," Reuters, December 18, 2017, https://www.reuters.com/article/us-cuba-russia-analysis/cuba-boosts-trade-ties-with-cold-war-ally-russia-as-u-s-disengages-idUSKBN1ED0FI.

32. Juan Pablo Duch, "Refrendan Cuba y Rusia etapa de cooperación bilateral más estrecha," *La Jornada*, November 3, 2018, http://www.jornada.com.mx/2018/11/03/mundo/020n1mun#W9.

33. "Statement by the President on Cuba Policy Changes," December 17, 2014, https://obamawhitehouse.archives.gov/the-press-office/2014/12/17/statement-president-cuba-policy-changes-0.

34. William M. LeoGrande, "Cuba Must Contend with a New Cold War in the Western Hemisphere," *World Politics Review*, January 24, 2019, https://www.worldpoliticsreview.com/articles/27270/cuba-must-contend-with-a-new-cold-war-in-the-western-hemisphere.

35. See "I've Been Very Proactive on Cuba: Trump," CNBC, https://www.cnbc.com/video/2018/09/26/ive-been-very-proactive-on-cuba-trump.html.

36. For an insightful and comprehensive summary of the evolution of Cuban foreign policy, see Carlos Alzugaray, "Cuban Revolutionary Diplomacy 1959–2017," based on his November 2017 presentation at Kanagawa University in Japan and subsequently published in *Medium*, https://medium.com/@Zuky43/cuban-revolutionary-diplomacy-1959-2017-1-c513c4effcOd.

37. "Cuban President Díaz-Canel Gives First Speech in Assembly," *Al Jazeera*, April 19, 2018, https://www.aljazeera.com/news/2018/04/miguel-diaz-canel-elect.

38. See a full analysis by H. Michael Erisman, "Cuba's International Economic Relations: "A Macroperspective on Performance and Challenges," in *Cuban Foreign Policy: Transformation under Raúl Castro*, ed. H. Michael Erisman and John M. Kirk (Lanham, MD: Rowman & Littlefield, 2018), 49.

39. Found at https://twitter.com/realdonaldtrump/status/1123333506346749952.

4. CUBAN SOCIETY

1. The number of "self-employed" ("trabajadores por cuenta propia") rose from 157,000 in 2010 to 593,000 in 2018. "Trabajo por cuenta propia: Se ratifican normas y se apruebaan importantes modificaciones," *Cubadebate*, http://www.cubadebate.cu/especiales/2018/10/03/que-desea-conocer-sobre-el-trabajo-por-cuenta-propia-en-cuba-infografias-y-video.

2. Claes Brundenius and Ricardo Torres Pérez, eds., *No More Free Lunch: Reflections on the Cuban Economic Reform Process and Challenges for Transformation* (Switzerland: Springer, 2013).

3. Hope Bastian, *Everyday Adjustments in Havana: Economic Reforms, Mobility, and Emerging Inequalities* (Lanham, MD: Lexington Books, 2018); M. Uriarte, "Social Impact of the Economic Measures," in *A Contemporary Cuba Reader: Reinventing the Revolution*, ed. Philip Brenner, Marguerite Rose Jiménez, John M. Kirk, and William M. LeoGrande (Lanham, MD: Rowman & Littlefield, 2007).

4. In this chapter the term "Afro-Cuban" is consciously used to include all Cubans who are phenotypically not white. Mayra Espina, "Viejas y nuevas desigualdades en Cuba," *Nueva Sociedad* 216 (July–August 2008): 133–149; María del Carmen Zabala, "Análisis de la dimensión racial en los procesos de reproducción de la pobreza. El rol de las políticas sociales

para favorecer la equidad social en Cuba," in *Pobreza, exclusión social y discriminación étnico-racial en América Latina y el Caribe*, ed. María del Carmen Zabala (Bogotá: Siglo del Hombre Editores, 2008), 397–423.

5. Alejandro de la Fuente, *A Nation for All: Race, Inequality, and Politics in Twentieth-Century Cuba* (Chapel Hill: University of North Carolina Press, 2011); A. Helg, *Our Rightful Share: The Afro-Cuban Struggle for Equality, 1886–1912* (Chapel Hill: University of North Carolina Press, 1995).

6. US Census Bureau, "The Hispanic Population 2010," 2010 Census Briefs, p. 14, last modified May 2011, https://www.census.gov/prod/cen2010/briefs/c2010br-04.pdf.

7. Emilio Morales, "Remittances to Cuba Diversify and Heat Up the Payment Channels," Havana Consulting Group, last modified March 3, 2011, http://www.thehavanaconsultinggroup.com/en/Articles/Article/63?Aspx

8. Sarah Blue, "The Erosion of Racial Equality in the Context of Cuba's Dual Economy," *Latin American Politics and Society* 49, no. 3 (2007): 35–68; K. Hansing and U. Optenhögel, "Las Desigualdades se Tornan Visibles: Consecuencias de la economía de escasez y reformas," *Nueva Sociedad* 255 (2015); K. Hansing and B. Hoffmann, "Cuba's New Social Structure: Assessing the Re-stratification of Cuban Society Sixty Years after Revolution" (Hamburg: GIGA Working Paper Series, 2019).

9. *Llega y pon* comes from *llegar*, "to come," and *poner*, "to put down or squat."

10. Yulexis Almeida Junco, "El acceso a la educación superior en Cuba: Breve reflexión desde la perspectiva racial," in Forum XXI, *Retos Docentes Universitarios como Desafío Curricular* (Madrid: McGraw-Hill Education, 2016).

11. "Especial sobre Internet en Cuba," *Periodismo de Barrio* (2018), https://www.periodismodebarrio.org/internetencuba.

12. B. Hoffmann, *The Politics of the Internet in Third World Development: Challenges in Contrasting Regimes with Case Studies of Costa Rica and Cuba* (New York: Routledge, 2004).

13. Kirk Semple and Hannah Berkeley Cohen, "Cuba Expands Private Internet Access," *New York Times*, July 30, 2019.

14. *Temas: Cultura Ideología Sociedad* 70 (April–June 2012): 81–91, http://www.temas.cult.cu/revista/70/democracia-y-sociedad.

15. John M. Kirk, "Surfing Revolico.com," in *A Contemporary Cuba Reader: The Revolution under Raúl Castro*, ed. Philip Brenner, Marguerite Rose Jiménez, John M. Kirk, and William M. LeoGrande (Lanham, MD: Rowman & Littlefield, 2014).

16. Ted A. Henken and Sjamme van de Voort, "From Cyberspace to Public Space? The Emergent Blogosphere and Cuban Civil Society," in *A Contemporary Cuba Reader: The Revolution under Raúl Castro*, ed. Philip Brenner, Marguerite Rose Jiménez, John M. Kirk, and William M. LeoGrande (Lanham, MD: Rowman & Littlefield, 2014).

17. Ted Henken, "Cuba's Digital Millennials: Independent Digital Media and Civil Society on the Island of the Disconnected," *Social Research: An International Quarterly* 84, no. 2 (2017): 429–56.

18. "Política y Lealtad a Cuba. Un debate," *Cuba Posible Cuadernos* 17 (La Habana, 2015), http://cubaposible.com/wp-content/uploads/2016/09/Cuaderno-17.-Politica-y-lealtad-a-Cuba.-Un-debate-Cuba-Posible.pdf.

19. Miguel Díaz-Canel, "Conferencia para cuadros del Partido Comunista" (2017), https://www.youtube.com/watch?v=l6cruK_KRzs.

20. Marie-Laure Geoffray, "Transnational Dynamics of Contention in Contemporary Cuba," *Journal of Latin American Studies* 42, no. 2 (2015): 223–49.

21. Andrea Rodríguez, "Cuba Softens New Law on Artistic Expression" *AP News*, December 6, 2018, https://www.apnews.com/f618c920e5a74d0b82a6c2cbb8184931.

Index

About the Editors and Contributors

Philip Brenner is professor of international relations, affiliate professor of history, and director of the graduate program in US foreign policy and national security at American University in Washington, DC. A specialist on US foreign policy toward Latin America, his most recent book, *Cuba Libre: A 500-Year Quest for Independence* (2018), was named a "A Best Book for 2018" by *Foreign Affairs* magazine.

John M. Kirk is professor of Latin American studies at Dalhousie University in Canada. He is the author/coeditor of several books on Cuba, dealing with José Martí, religion and politics, culture, and international relations. His most recent works are *Healthcare without Borders: Understanding Cuban Medical Internationalism* (2015) and *Cuban Foreign Policy: Transformation under Raúl Castro* (2018). He has been travelling to Cuba regularly since 1976.

William M. LeoGrande is professor of government in the School of Public Affairs at American University in Washington, DC. He specializes in Latin American politics and US relations with Latin America, with a particular focus on Cuba. He has written for a wide range of scholarly and popular publications and is coauthor of *Back Channel to Cuba: The Hidden History of Negotiations between Washington and Havana*.

Katrin Hansing is associate professor of anthropology at the City University of New York (CUNY) and senior research fellow at the German Institute for Global and Area Studies (GIGA). Since the 1990s she has conducted extensive research and published widely on different aspects of Cuban society and culture.

Bert Hoffmann is a Latin America expert at the German Institute for Global and Area Studies (GIGA), head of the GIGA Berlin office, and professor of political science at Freie Universität Berlin. He has published widely on the social, political, and economic transformation of Cuba since the early 1990s.

Ricardo Torres Pérez is professor and deputy director of the Centro de Estudios de la Economía Cubana at the University of Havana. Editor-in-chief of the series *Miradas a la Economía Cubana* (Views on the Cuban Economy), Dr. Torres is also the principal Cuban researcher for the *Econolatin* network and a columnist for *Progreso Semanal/Progreso Weekly*. He is the coeditor of *No More Free Lunch: Reflections on the Cuban Economic Reform Process and Challenges for Transformation* (2014).